INSTANT OMNI PLUS AIR FRYER TOASTER OVEN COOKBOOK

110 EASY, HEALTHY AND EFFORTLESS RECIPES WHICH ANYONE CAN COOK ON A BUDGET.

DANA REED

CONTENTS

RED MEAT RECIPES

SEAFOOD RECIPES

VEGAN & VEGETARIAN RECIPES

APPETIZERS RECIPES

SNACKS AND DESSERTS

BREAD, PIZZAS AND CAKES

INTRODUCTION

Instant Omni air fryer toaster oven is an excellent appliance that can be used for home cooking some fantastic and nutritious meals every day with ease of access. It is an appliance that can turn on with the touch of a button. The instant Omni plus air fryer toaster oven is 26 liter in the capacity that is large enough to compensate a lot of cooking, including slow cook, roast, dehydrate, rotisserie cook, and of course toast.

The instant Omni plus air fryer toaster oven is large enough to cook a large quantity of food, that feeds your whole family and your friends. The instant Omni air fryer has a golden Quartz technology that has a high heating performance and dual top and bottom heating elements, and both of these results in some Golden and crispy meal that is prepared in few seconds every time.

The instant Omni air fryer offers one-click technology that allows the user to start the cooking with a touch of a button and forget about calculating time, weight, or temperature.

You can select any of the options from its 11 smart programs, according to your cooking needs.

If you are a foodie and into making some different and versatile recipes, that ask for a different method of cooking, then Omni fryer toaster oven provides you the flexibility to adjust the setting and customize your culinary experience.

The instant Omni Plus is much more than a toaster and it comes with all of the necessary accessories that you need to perform the rotisserie cooking.

It is a high-performance toaster oven with a lot of other functions that deliver some tender mouth-watering aromatic and delicious meals.

Essentials of Instant Omni Plus Air Fryer Toaster Oven

The instant Omni plus air fryer toaster oven is a terrific cooking appliance that makes the cooking easy by circulating hot air around the food. It is no doubt another hit multi-user kitchen an appliance by the instant pot, that changed the way cooking was done before at home. Now you don't need to buy a different cooking appliance, as this remarkable appliance has functions of 11 appliances.

11 In 1 Appliance

The instant Omni plus is a multi-cooker toaster oven that provides two cooking methods with nine smart programs.

1. These nine programs include:
2. 1.Dehydrate
3. 2.Proof
4. 3.Toast
5. 4.Bake
6. 5.Air Fry
7. 6.Slow-Cook
8. 7.Roast
9. 8.Reheat
10. 9.Rotate
11. 10.Convect
12. 11. Broil

Dual Heating Elements

Air fryer toaster oven heating elements are positioned on the top and the bottom of the Omni toaster oven. Along with that, there is an option to use the conjunction that makes the cooking even on all sides.

Large Capacity

Instant Omni air fryer is 26 liter in the capacity with its sleek stainless steel and clean finish.

Now you can cook different types of recipes using an instant Omni air fryer like a pro.

This toaster oven surely satisfies all your cooking needs.

Healthy Meals

The food cooked using air fryer not only prepped with a single button touch but also cooked in less amount of oil. Its technology locks the flavor and nutrients without adding any extra fat. No doubt, instant Omni air fryer makes the cooking easy.

BRUNCHES

1

STRAWBERRY TURNOVERS

It is a very easy recipe that can be prepared with leftovers.

Preparation Time: 15 Minutes

Cooking Time: 15 Minutes

Yield: 2 Servings

Ingredients

- 1 cup Strawberry Pie filling
- 1 Puff Pastry
- 1/3 cup icing sugar
- Cooking Spray

Directions

1.Take a puff pastry and lay it onto a flat surface.

2.Cut the pastry into 4 equal squares.

3.Top each square with the spoonful of strawberry filling, but on the corners of pastry.

4.Fold it into a triangle shape and press the edges.

5.Spray it with cooking spray.

6.Layer it on an Instant Omni plus air fryer toaster oven basket and then air fry for 15 minutes at 350 degrees Fahrenheit.

7.Once done, serve and enjoy with a sprinkle of icing sugar on top.

Nutrition Facts
Servings: 2
Amount per serving
Calories 260
% Daily Value*
Total Fat 9.3g 12%
Saturated Fat 2.3g 12%
Cholesterol 0mg 0%
Sodium 71mg 3%
Total Carbohydrate 42g 15%
Dietary Fiber 0.8g 3%
Total Sugars 29.3g
Protein 1.7g
Vitamin D 0mcg 0%
Calcium 3mg 0%
Iron 1mg 4%
Potassium 15mg 0%

2

SWEET POTATO ORANGE CUPS

It is a very versatile brunch recipe that is prepared with readily available ingredients.

Preparation Time: 20 Minutes

Cooking Time: 5 Minutes

Yield: 4 Servings

Ingredients

- 4 large sweet potatoes
- 1/2 cup brown sugar packed
- 1/4 cup half-and-half cream
- 4 tablespoons butter
- 3/4 cup miniature marshmallows
- 4 large oranges halved, medium size

Directions

1. Take a saucepan and put sweet potatoes in it.

2. Put the generous amount of water in the saucepan and boil the sweet potatoes.

3. Cook for about 25 minutes until the potatoes get soft and tender.

4. Take a large bowl and mashed sweet potatoes in it.

5. Then add sugar, cream, butter, and marshmallows in it.

6.Take the oranges and cut them in half.

7.Remove the pulp from the oranges and leave the shells.

8.Now put the spoon full of potato mixture into the oranges shell.

9.Air fry it for 5 minutes, in Instant Omni plus air fryer toaster oven ,at 340 degrees Fahrenheit.

10. Once it's done serve.

Nutrition Facts

Servings: 4

Amount per serving

Calories 322

% Daily Value*

Total Fat 13.5g 17%

Saturated Fat 8.4g 42%

Cholesterol 36mg 12%

Sodium 104mg 5%

Total Carbohydrate 51.2g 19%

Dietary Fiber 4.4g 16%

Total Sugars 41.4g

Protein 2.4g

Vitamin D 8mcg 40%

Calcium 108mg 8%

Iron 0mg 2%

Potassium 381mg 8%

3

CINNAMON ROLLS

It is a very simple yet classic treat that is perfectly served at brunch time.

Preparation Time: 10 Minutes

Cooking Time: 8 Minutes

Yield: 2 Servings

Ingredients

- 1 can cinnamon rolls
- Oil spray, for greasing
- Icing sugar, topping

Directions

1. Remove the cinnamon roll from the package.

2. Place on the oil greased air fryer rack.

3. Cook for 8 minutes in Instant Omni plus air fryer toaster oven.

4. Add a minute or two if not firm, when you touch.

5. Top it with icing and serve.

Nutrition Facts

Servings: 2

Amount per serving

Calories 130

% Daily Value*
Total Fat 5.2g 7%
Saturated Fat 1g 5%
Cholesterol 20mg 7%
Sodium 115mg 5%
Total Carbohydrate 19.3g 7%
Dietary Fiber 0.7g 3%
Total Sugars 13.4g
Protein 1.9g
Vitamin D 0mcg 0%
Calcium 22mg 2%
Iron 0mg 3%
Potassium 33mg 1%

4

SAUSAGE ROLL-UPS

It is a simple yet delicious brunch recipe, loved by whole family members.

Preparation Time: 10 Minutes
Cooking Time: 15-20 Minutes
Yield: 5 Servings
Ingredients
- 10 sausage links, cooked
- 10 brown bread slices
- 4 organic eggs, whisked
- 1/2 cup almond milk
- 1 teaspoon vanilla extract
- 1/2 teaspoon cinnamon, grounded
- 1/4 teaspoon of nutmeg, ground
- Maple syrup, side serving
- Ketchup, side serving

Directions
1.First, cut the bread slices edges.
2.Now, roll one sausage in one bread slice.
3.Continue the process until all the sausages are rolled up.
4.Take a medium bowl and whisk eggs in it.

5.Then add almond milk, vanilla, nutmeg, and cinnamon, beat until combined.

6.Dip each roll into the egg mixture and then place it in an Instant Omni plus air fryer toaster oven tray.

7.Now set the a temperate to 375 degrees F, and put the tray inside the oven rack.

8.Remember to cook the bread slices in batches according to the air fryer toaster oven capacity,

9.Cook for 5 minutes, for each batch.

10. Once done, serve hot with a drizzle of maple syrup or even ketchup, and enjoy as a delicious brunch.

Nutrition Facts

Servings: 5

Amount per serving

Calories 660

% Daily Value*

Total Fat 21.1g 27%

Saturated Fat 10g 50%

Cholesterol 150mg 50%

Sodium 1158mg 50%

Total Carbohydrate 90g 33%

Dietary Fiber 11.7g 42%

Total Sugars 7.5g

Protein 27.2g

Vitamin D 12mcg 62%

Calcium 29mg 2%

Iron 1mg 7%

Potassium 267mg

5

STRAWBERRY SHORTCAKE TOASTS

It is a fun easy kid loving brunch recipe, which offers great taste. The addition of fruits makes it a healthy meal to enjoy at brunch.

Preparation Time: 15 Minutes

Cooking Time: 10-20 Minutes

Yield: 4 Servings

Ingredients

- 8 slices of French bread
- 8 ounces room temperature cream cheese
- 1/4 cup sugar
- 4 eggs
- 1 cup half and half
- 1 teaspoon vanilla extract
- 4 Strawberries, topping
- 1/2 cup Whipped Cream, topping
- Oil spray, for greasing

Directions

1.Coat an Instant Omni plus air fryer toaster oven safe pan with oil spray.

2.In a bowl mix together cream cheese and sugar.

3.Spread cream mixture on one side of the bread and then put bread on top to make a sandwich, then press down a bit.

4.Place bread slice in pan.

5.Whisk egg in a bowl and add vanilla and half and half.

6.Mix well and then pour it over the bread.

7.Cover the pan and refrigerate for 4 hours.

8.Now, set the Instant Omni plus air fryer toaster oven to 5 minutes, at 330 degrees F.

9.Put the bread pan in the air fryer for cooking, once time completes, flip the French toasts and cook for another side for 5 more minutes.

10. Top with whipped cream and strawberries.

11. Enjoy.

Nutrition Facts

Servings: 4

Amount per serving

Calories 623

% Daily Value*

Total Fat 37.1g 48%

Saturated Fat 21.4g 107%

Cholesterol 265mg 88%

Sodium 675mg 29%

Total Carbohydrate 54.6g 20%

Dietary Fiber 1.8g 6%

Total Sugars 15.4g

Protein 19.5g

Vitamin D 15mcg 77%

Calcium 173mg 13%

Iron 4mg 22%

Potassium 321mg 7%

6

HEAVENLY FRENCH TOASTS

It is a perfect brunch-time meal that is absolute love.

Preparation Time: 10 Minutes

Cooking Time: 6 Minutes

Yield: 3 Servings

Ingredients

- 6 bread slices
- 4 eggs
- 1/2 cup milk
- 1 teaspoon of vanilla extract
- 1/2 teaspoon of cinnamon

Directions

1.Take a medium bowl and whisk eggs in it then add vanilla, cinnamon, and milk.

2.Whisk well for fine combining.

3.Dip each bread piece in the mixture then shake off excess liquid.

4.Put pieces in the pan.

5.Put the pan in the Instant Omni plus air fryer toaster oven.

6.Air fryer it for 3 minutes, at 340 degrees F.

7.Once the time of cooking completes, flip the bread to cook from the other side for more than 3 minutes.

8.Once it's done serve with maple syrup.

Nutrition Facts

Servings: 3

Amount per serving

Calories 154

% Daily Value*

Total Fat 6.8g 9%

Saturated Fat 2.2g 11%

Cholesterol 220mg 73%

Sodium 223mg 10%

Total Carbohydrate 12.1g 4%

Dietary Fiber 0.6g 2%

Total Sugars 3.5g

Protein 10.2g

Vitamin D 42mcg 208%

Calcium 111mg 9%

Iron 2mg 10%

Potassium 161mg 3%

7

ENGLISH BREAKFAST SCONES

These are mouthwatering, fluff, and wicked scones you ever tried, as we use instant pot Omni to make the cooking process much healthier.

Preparation Time: 10 Minutes
Cooking Time: 15 Minutes
Yield: 4 Servings
Ingredients
- 2 cups all-purpose flour or whole wheat flour
- 1/4 cup granulated white sugar
- 1 tablespoon of baking power
- 1/2 teaspoon baking soda
- 1/4 teaspoon salt
- 1/2 cup cold butter, cut into pieces more
- 1 egg more
- 1/2 cup buttermilk

Topping Ingredients
- 1 tablespoon buttermilk
- 2 teaspoons granulated sugar

Directions

1.Take a bowl and mix flour, baking powder, baking soda, salt, and sugar.

2.Add butter in pieces to the bowl and use a pastry blender to make crumbs of the mixture.

3.In a separate bowl beat the eggs and add milk, add dry ingredients into the egg mixture.

4.Make the dough and knead gently four times.

5.Brush it with some additional buttermilk and eggs wash.

6.Turn the Instant Omni plus air fryer toaster oven to 375°F for 15 minutes by pressing air fry.

7.Place the cooking pan into the oven.

8.Once the cooking is complete let the scones sit in the oven for 5-7 minutes.

9.Then take out and serve.

Nutrition Facts

Servings: 4

Amount per serving

Calories 306

% Daily Value*

Total Fat 2.2g 3%

Saturated Fat 0.7g 3%

Cholesterol 48mg 16%

Sodium 389mg 17%

Total Carbohydrate 57.6g 21%

Dietary Fiber 1.7g 6%

Total Sugars 10.1g

Protein 12.4g

Vitamin D 4mcg 22%

Calcium 57mg 4%

Iron 3mg 18%

Potassium 183mg 4%

8

TURKEY AND CHEESE SANDWICH

Looking for something cheesy during brunch time, then try our grilled cheese sandwich made in Omni air fryer toaster oven.

Preparation Time: 10 Minutes

Cooking Time: 6 Minutes

Yield: 3 Servings

Ingredients

- 2 slices bread
- 2 teaspoons butter
- 2 slices cheddar cheese
- 2 slices of turkey

Directions

1.Preheat the Instant Omni plus air fryer toaster oven at 350 degrees F.

2.Spread the butter on one side of bread and top it with cheese slice, and turkey.

3.Cover it with another bread slice and make a sandwich.

4.Put butter with a knife evenly on the outer surface of bread as well.

5.Put the sandwich inside the Instant Omni plus air fryer toaster oven baking tray.

6.Set the time for 5-6 minutes.

7.Turn the sandwich halfway.

8.Then serve and enjoy.

Nutrition Facts

Servings: 3

Amount per serving

Calories 349

% Daily Value*

Total Fat 15.9g 20%

Saturated Fat 7.9g 39%

Cholesterol 131mg 44%

Sodium 272mg 12%

Total Carbohydrate 3.3g 1%

Dietary Fiber 0.1g 1%

Total Sugars 0.4g

Protein 45.8g

Vitamin D 4mcg 20%

Calcium 148mg 11%

Iron 14mg 79%

Potassium 438mg 9%

9

CLASSIC BRUNCH BREAD

We use Instant Omni plus air fryer toaster oven that makes it a less greasy version.

Preparation Time: 30 Minutes

Cooking Time: 25 Minutes

Yield: 4 Servings

Ingredients

- 2 tablespoons of unsalted butter
- 1-1/2 teaspoon active yeast
- 1 teaspoon of sugar
- Pinch of salt
- 2 cups of Water
- 2-1/2 cups all-purpose flour

Directions

1.Use a stand mixer to beat together butter, sugar, salt, yeast, and water.

2.Mix it at high speed.

3.Then add 1/2 cup of flour at a time.

4.Then add all the flour and keep on mixing at medium speed for 5 minutes.

5.Once the dough is ready, take it out on the greased baking pan.

6.Wrap the dough with plastic wrapper, and then arrange a drip pan on the bottom of the Instant Omni plus air fryer toaster oven.

7.Place the baking pan over the dripping pan.

8.Now select bake at 400 degrees F.

9.Set timer to 25 minutes and press start.

10. Once the timer completes, remove the pan and set on a cooling rack for a few minutes, then slice and serve.

Nutrition Facts

Servings: 4

Amount per serving

Calories 285

% Daily Value*

Total Fat 6.4g 8%

Saturated Fat 3.8g 19%

Cholesterol 15mg 5%

Sodium 85mg 4%

Total Carbohydrate 49.1g 18%

Dietary Fiber 1.9g 7%

Total Sugars 1.2g

Protein 6.9g

Vitamin D 4mcg 20%

Calcium 15mg 1%

Iron 3mg 17%

Potassium 90mg 2%

10

INSTANT OMNI PLUS AIR FRYER TOASTER OVEN PIZZA

Set aside the frozen pizza, and make one fresh and healthy pizza for brunch.

Preparation Time: 15 Minutes

Cooking Time: 10 Minutes

Yield: Servings

Ingredients

- 1/2 cup of Buffalo mozzarella
- 12 inches of Pizza dough
- 2 tablespoons of Olive oil
- 1/2 cup of Tomato sauce
- Few basil leaves
- 1 teaspoon of pepper flakes
- Oil spray, for greasing

Directions

1.Preheat the Instant Omni plus air fryer toaster oven to 375 degrees F.

2.Spray the air fryer basket with oil spray.

3.Now, pat the mozzarella cheese with a paper towel.

4.Roll the pizza dough to the size of the air fryer tray.

5.Slightly brush it with olive oil from the top and then put mozzarella cheese, tomato sauce ad few basil leaves on top.

6.Bake it for 10 minutes, in Instant Omni plus air fryer toaster oven ,until cheese melts.

7.Serve with a seasoning of red chili flakes.

Nutrition Facts

Servings: 4

Amount per serving

Calories 422

% Daily Value*

Total Fat 30.2g 39%

Saturated Fat 7g 35%

Cholesterol 2mg 1%

Sodium 577mg 25%

Total Carbohydrate 32.9g 12%

Dietary Fiber 3g 11%

Total Sugars 1.1g

Protein 5.2g

Vitamin D 0mcg 0%

Calcium 9mg 1%

Iron 2mg 10%

Potassium 123mg 3%

11

AIR FRYER POCKETS

It is a very versatile recipe to enjoy any time you liked.

Preparation Time: 15 Minutes

Cooking Time: 6 Minutes

Yield: 1 Serving

Ingredients

- 2 slices of bread
- 2 eggs
- 1/2 cup milk
- 1/4 cup cream cheese
- 2 frozen strawberries, chopped

Directions

1. Mix strawberries and cream cheese in a bowl to make the filling.

2. Use a rolling pin to flatten the bread slices.

3. Now use a teaspoon of strawberry filling to fill the center of the bread slice.

4. Place another piece of bread on top and press down from the edges to seal.

5. In a bowl, whisk together the egg and milk.

6. Dip the toast into the egg and milk mixture.

7.Then place in a Instant Omni plus air fryer toaster oven greased tray.

8.Put the tray inside the fryer toaster oven.

9.Cook at 350 degrees F for 6 minutes in Instant Omni plus air fryer toaster oven.

10. Then serve and enjoy.

Nutrition Facts

Servings: 1

Amount per serving

Calories 443

% Daily Value*

Total Fat 32.1g 41%

Saturated Fat 17.1g 86%

Cholesterol 401mg 134%

Sodium 475mg 21%

Total Carbohydrate 19g 7%

Dietary Fiber 0.8g 3%

Total Sugars 8.2g

Protein 20.8g

Vitamin D 31mcg 157%

Calcium 268mg 21%

Iron 3mg 17%

Potassium 275mg 6%

TOASTED BAGEL FOR BRUNCH

It is a hit recipe that is lover by all.

Preparation Time: 5 Minutes

Cooking Time: 2 Minutes

Yield: 1 Serving

Ingredients

- 1 bagel
- 5 tablespoons of cream cheese

Directions

1.The first step is to slice the bagel and then place it inside an Instant Omni plus air fryer toaster oven tray.

2.Turn on the broiler button and set for 1 minute.

3.Take out the tray.

4.Add butter on top of the bagel and then again put back in the oven to broil for 1 minute.

5.Once done, serve with cream cheese topping.

Nutrition Facts

Servings: 1

Amount per serving

Calories 320

% Daily Value*

Total Fat 18.4g 24%
Saturated Fat 11.2g 56%
Cholesterol 55mg 18%
Sodium 402mg 17%
Total Carbohydrate 30g 11%
Dietary Fiber 1.3g 4%
Total Sugars 3g
Protein 9.5g
Vitamin D 0mcg 0%
Calcium 90mg 7%
Iron 4mg 22%
Potassium 102mg 2%

13

GRILL CHEESE SANDWICH

It is a cheesy and delicious recipe to enjoy.

Preparation Time: 5 Minutes

Cooking Time: 10 Minutes

Yield: 1 Serving

Ingredients

- 4 slices white bread
- 2 tablespoons of butter softened
- 2 slices cheddar, provolone

Directions

1.The first step is to butter the two bread slices and then place butter side down on an Instant Omni plus air fryer toaster oven cooking tray.

2.Top each bread with chess slice.

3.Now butter remaining bread slices and put it on top of cheese slices.

4.Remember to put the drip pan in the bottom of the cooking tray.

5.Now select AIRFRY, and then select the temperature to 375 degrees for 10 minutes.

6.Once the cooking cycle complete, take out the sandwich and enjoy warm.

Nutrition Facts

Servings: 1

Amount per serving

Calories 396

% Daily Value*

Total Fat 28.1g 36%

Saturated Fat 17.3g 86%

Cholesterol 73mg 24%

Sodium 751mg 33%

Total Carbohydrate 19.3g 7%

Dietary Fiber 0.9g 3%

Total Sugars 1.9g

Protein 16.6g

Vitamin D 16mcg 80%

Calcium 294mg 23%

Iron 2mg 9%

Potassium 80mg 2%

BACON IN OMNI AIR FRYER TOASTER

It is a very easy and simple way to make bacon using the Omni air fryer toaster oven.

Preparation Time: 5 Minutes

Cooking Time: 10 Minutes

Yield: 2 Servings

Ingredients

- 1 package bacon, personal preference

Directions

1.Preheat the Instant Omni plus air fryer toaster oven for 5 minutes.

2.Layout the bacon in the preheated air fryer, by adding it to the tray.

3.Put the try in the Instant Omni plus air fryer toaster oven and set it to 5 minutes at 400 degrees F.

4.Flip after 5 minutes and cook for 5 more minutes.

5.Plate and serve.

6.Enjoy.

Nutrition Facts

Servings: 2

Amount per serving

Calories 344
% Daily Value*
Total Fat 26.5g 34%
Saturated Fat 8.7g 44%
Cholesterol 70mg 23%
Sodium 1467mg 64%
Total Carbohydrate 0.9g 0%
Dietary Fiber 0g 0%
Total Sugars 0g
Protein 23.5g
Vitamin D 0mcg 0%
Calcium 7mg 1%
Iron 1mg 5%
Potassium 359mg 8%

15

HONEY GLAZED SWEET POTATOES

It is a very good alternative to hash brown when having a brunch.

Preparation Time: 20 Minutes

Cooking Time: 25 Minutes

Yield: 2 Servings

Ingredients

- 2 medium sweet potatoes
- 1 teaspoon olive oil extra virgin
- 2 teaspoons raw honey
- 1 teaspoon cinnamon
- Pinch of salt

Directions

1.Wash and peel the sweet potatoes and dice it to even cubes.

2.In a bowl mix honey, olive oil, cinnamon, and salt.

3.Toss the cubes of sweet potatoes in bowl mixture, for fine coating.

4.Add sweet potatoes to Instant Omni plus air fryer toaster oven basket and cook on 400 for 20-25 minutes.

5.Remove it from the Instant Omni plus air fryer toaster oven ,and let the sweet potatoes rest for 10 minutes.

6.Serve and Enjoy.

Nutrition Facts
Servings: 2
Amount per serving
Calories 270
% Daily Value*
Total Fat 2.6g 3%
Saturated Fat 0.4g 2%
Cholesterol 0mg 0%
Sodium 91mg 4%
Total Carbohydrate 59.8g 22%
Dietary Fiber 6.8g 24%
Total Sugars 17.8g
Protein 2.4g
Vitamin D 0mcg 0%
Calcium 37mg 3%
Iron 1mg 5%
Potassium 1229mg 26%

POULTRY RECIPES

16

AIR FRYER FROZEN CHICKEN DRUMSTICKS

It is one of the best and exciting chicken recipes to enjoy.

Preparation Time: 25 Minutes

Cooking Time: 20 Minutes

Yields: 4 Servings

Ingredients

- 2 pounds of chicken drumsticks, frozen
- 2 tablespoons of olive oil
- Salt and black pepper, to taste
- 1 teaspoon of garlic powder
- 1 teaspoon paprika
- 1 teaspoon onion powder

Directions

1. Take a large bowl and add drumsticks in it.

2. Drizzle the olive oil on top and rub the drum stick with the olive oil coating generously.

3. Then rub the drum stick with seasoning including salt, pepper, garlic powder, paprika, and onion powder.

4. Marinate the dumbstruck in the refrigerator for 2 hours.

5. Afterward, take out the drumstick and place them in the air fryer basket.

6.Cook for 20 minutes at 375 degrees F inside Instant Omni plus air fryer toaster oven.

7.Serve and enjoy.

Nutrition Facts

Servings: 4

Amount per serving

Calories 449

% Daily Value*

Total Fat 20g 26%

Saturated Fat 4.4g 22%

Cholesterol 200mg 67%

Sodium 182mg 8%

Total Carbohydrate 1.3g 0%

Dietary Fiber 0.3g 1%

Total Sugars 0.4g

Protein 62.6g

Vitamin D 0mcg 0%

Calcium 29mg 2%

Iron 3mg 18%

Potassium 478mg 10%

17

AIR FRYER STUFFED CHICKEN BREAST

If you are looking for a yummy chicken recipe then this serves the purpose.

Preparation Time: 25 Minutes

Cooking Time: 20 Minutes

Yields: 2 Servings

Ingredients

- 2 chicken breasts
- Salt and black pepper, to taste
- 1/4 cup apple peeled and diced
- 1/2 cup shredded cheddar cheese
- 2 tablespoons fine bread crumbs
- 2 tablespoons butter
- 1 cup chicken broth

Directions

1.Take a bowl and combined apple, butter, cheese, and bread crumbs.

2.Rub the chicken with salt and black pepper.

3.Butterfly cut the chicken breast pieces and fills the center with a prepared bowl apple mixture.

4.Secure the chicken breast pieces with a toothpick.

5.Take a shallow baking pan and place chicken in it along with the chicken broth.

6.Cover it with foil.

7.Cook for 20 minutes at 350 degrees Fahrenheit, inside an Instant Omni plus air fryer toaster oven.

8.Once done remove it from the air fryer.

9.Serve.

Nutrition Facts

Servings: 2

Amount per serving

Calories 463

% Daily Value*

Total Fat 23.7g 30%

Saturated Fat 10.6g 53%

Cholesterol 160mg 53%

Sodium 698mg 30%

Total Carbohydrate 13.6g 5%

Dietary Fiber 1.2g 4%

Total Sugars 4.1g

Protein 46.4g

Vitamin D 8mcg 40%

Calcium 56mg 4%

Iron 3mg 16%

Potassium 514mg 11%.

18

WHOLE CHICKEN

It is a very simple and mouthwatering chicken recipe that can be prepared using an Omni air fryer.

Preparation Time: 25 Minutes

Cooking Time: 60 Minutes

Yields: 4 Servings

Ingredients

- 1 Whole Chicken, 4 pounds, cut in 4 large pieces
- 1 tablespoon paprika
- Salt and black pepper, to taste
- 2 tablespoons olive oil

Directions

1. Wash and pat dry the chicken.

2. Rub chicken with olive oil and seasoning.

3. Preheat the a Instant Omni plus air fryer toaster oven to 350 degrees F.

4. Bake it for 60 minutes or until the temperature is 165 Degrees F.

5. Serve.

Nutrition Facts

Servings: 4

Amount per serving

Calories 342

% Daily Value*

Total Fat 18g 23%

Saturated Fat 4g 20%

Cholesterol 130mg 43%

Sodium 126mg 5%

Total Carbohydrate 1g 0%

Dietary Fiber 0.7g 2%

Total Sugars 0.2g

Protein 42.5g

Vitamin D 0mcg 0%

Calcium 25mg 2%

Iron 2mg 12%

Potassium 396mg 8%

19

AIR FRYER ROTISSERIE CHICKEN

It is a great tasting chicken recipe that is prepared using an instant Omni air fryer oven. The chicken is cooked to its crispy tender perfection.

Preparation Time: 25 Minutes
Cooking Time: 30 Minutes
Yield: 4 Servings
Ingredients
- 2 pounds of a whole chicken, cut in a piece
- Salt and black pepper
- 3 tablespoons of avocado oil
- 1 teaspoon of thyme, dried
- 1 tablespoon Italian seasoning
- 2 teaspoons garlic powder
- 2 teaspoons onion powder
- 1 teaspoon paprika

Directions
1.Wash and pat dry the chicken pieces.
2.Take a small bowl and combine all the listed ingredients in it, excluding the chicken.
3.Mix well and set aside.

4.Run the chicken with the prepared marinade.

5.Marinate the chicken in the spices for 2 hours.

6.Afterward, put the chicken pieces in air fryer, use rotisserie functions and tool to cook the chicken.

7.Turn on the Instant Omni plus air fryer toaster oven at 400 degrees for 30 minutes.

8.After 10 minutes flip the chicken and then complete the cooking for 20 minutes.

9.Once done, serve hot.

10. Note: The chicken of about 4-5 pounds can be cooked easily in one batch by putting it directly on a rotisserie and a rack .the rack below rotisserie serves as dripping pan as well.

11. Remember to put the foil on top of the rack and place pieces according to capacity. The bottom of the oven can also be used to cook chicken directly, just remember to cover it with aluminum foil.

Nutrition Facts

Servings: 4

Amount per serving

Calories 467

% Daily Value*

Total Fat 19.3g 25%

Saturated Fat 5.1g 25%

Cholesterol 204mg 68%

Sodium 198mg 9%

Total Carbohydrate 3.4g 1%

Dietary Fiber 1g 3%

Total Sugars 1.2g

Protein 66.2g

Vitamin D 0mcg 0%

Calcium 46mg 4%

Iron 3mg 18%

Potassium 628mg 13%

20

TURKEY BREASTS

The recipes call for boneless turkey breasts that are roasted nicely using an Omni air fryer toaster oven. It is one of the easy and simple recipes to prepare anytime you like.

Preparation Time: 25 Minutes

Cooking Time: 30 Minutes

Yield: 4 Servings

Ingredients

- 2 pounds of turkey breast,
- 2 tablespoons of poultry rub seasoning
- 2 tablespoons of olive oil

Directions

1.First, rub the turkey with olive oil and then coat it with dry rub seasoning.

2.Tie the turkey breast to keep it compact.

3.Place the breast in the air fryer basket, and put it in the air fryer.

4.Air Fry for 30 minutes at 380 degrees F.

5.Turn the meat as needed during the cooking process.

6.Let the breast rest for 5-10 minutes, before taking out.

7.Remember to cook the chicken in batches according to air fryer oven space.

8.Crave and serve the turkey breasts.

Nutrition Facts

Servings: 4

Amount per serving

Calories 302

% Daily Value*

Total Fat 10.9g 14%

Saturated Fat 1.8g 9%

Cholesterol 98mg 33%

Sodium 2303mg 100%

Total Carbohydrate 10.8g 4%

Dietary Fiber 1.3g 5%

Total Sugars 8g

Protein 38.9g

Vitamin D 0mcg 0%

Calcium 37mg 3%

Iron 4mg 22%

Potassium 698mg 15%

21

AIR FRYER SOUTHERN FRIED CHICKEN

If you want to have a true taste of southern fried chicken with no overcooking, then try this recipe that gives you the same taste as it came out of a deep fryer.

Preparation Time: 20 Minutes
Cooking Time: 30 Minutes
Yield: 3 Servings
Ingredients

- 6 chicken drumsticks
- Salt, to taste
- Black pepper, to taste
- 1 teaspoon of avocado oil
- 1 teaspoon Onion Powder
- 1 teaspoon of paprika
- 1 teaspoon of garlic powder
- 2 eggs
- 2 tablespoons of milk
- 1-1/2 cup Flour
- 1/4 cup Corn Starch
- Oil spray, for coating

- 2 tablespoons of poultry seasoning, dry

Directions

1.Rub the chicken pieces with salt and black pepper.

2.Then rub avocado oil all over the chicken.

3.Take a bowl and mix onion powder, paprika, and garlic powder.

4.Put the chicken in a bowl and let the species coat the meat.

5.Take a bowl and mix flour, cornstarch, and poultry seasoning.

6.In a separate bowl, whisk eggs and add milk.

7.Take a piece of chicken and roll it in the egg mixture then in flour mixture.

8.Shake off excess flour.

9.Repeat with all the chicken pieces.

10. Now as we are using air fryer so it's necessary to spray the chicken pieces with olive oil spray, else you will get a powdered chicken, as the flour will not get moist.

11. Place the chicken pieces on the baking tray, according to capacity.

12. Air fry it for 30 minutes, at 400 degrees F, inside an Instant Omni plus air fryer toaster oven.

13. Once done, serve and enjoy.

Nutrition Facts

Servings: 3

Amount per serving

Calories 496

% Daily Value*

Total Fat 9.7g 12%

Saturated Fat 2.7g 13%

Cholesterol 191mg 64%

Sodium 173mg 8%

Total Carbohydrate 63.9g 23%

Dietary Fiber 2.5g 9%

Total Sugars 1.5g

Protein 36.4g

Vitamin D 10mcg 52%
Calcium 77mg 6%
Iron 6mg 32%
Potassium 351mg 7%

22

TANDOORI CHICKEN RECIPE

A true taste of authentic tandoori chicken is introduced in this recipe, with the addition of yogurt-based spice blends.

Preparation Time: 15 Minute

Cooking Time: 20 Minutes

Yield: 3 Servings

Ingredients

- 1-1/2 pound chicken drumsticks

Ingredients for Marinade

- 1 cup plain Greek yogurt
- 1 teaspoon ginger, minced
- 3 teaspoons garlic, minced
- 3 tablespoons olive oil
- 2 tablespoons lemon juice
- Salt and black pepper, to taste
- 1/2 teaspoon turmeric powder
- 3 teaspoons Garam Masala
- 2 tablespoons coriander powder
- 2 teaspoons cumin powder
- 1/2 teaspoon red chili powder
- 2 teaspoons paprika

- 1 teaspoon fenugreek leaves, dried

Garnish Ingredients

- 1 teaspoon fresh lemon wedges

Directions

1.Take a large bowl and combine all the listed marinade ingredients in it.

2.Add chicken to the marinade and transfer it to a zip-lock plastic bag.

3.Let the chicken marinatefor2 hours in a refrigerator.

4.Take out the chicken 20 minutes, before cooking.

5.Now, put the chicken pieces in an Instant Omni plus air fryer toaster oven basket and air fry for 20 minutes at 400 degrees F.

6.Afterward, pull out the basket and flip the chicken and cook for 10 more minutes.

7.Once the internal temperature reaches 165 degrees F it's done, serve with a garnish of lemon wedges.

Nutrition Facts

Servings: 3

Amount per serving

Calories 561

% Daily Value*

Total Fat 27.8g 36%

Saturated Fat 5.6g 28%

Cholesterol 201mg 67%

Sodium 212mg 9%

Total Carbohydrate 8.2g 3%

Dietary Fiber 1.4g 5%

Total Sugars 3.5g

Protein 67.6g

Vitamin D 0mcg 0%

Calcium 102mg 8%

Iron 5mg 30%

Potassium 572mg 12%

23

AIR FRYER CHICKEN THIGHS

It is a very simple, quick, easy chicken thighs recipe, which is crispy outside and tender inside.

Preparation Time: 20 Minutes

Cooking Time: 28 Minutes

Yield: 1-2 Servings

Ingredients

- 4 skins-on, boneless chicken thighs
- 3 teaspoons extra-virgin olive oil
- 1/2 teaspoon smoked paprika
- 1 teaspoon garlic powder
- Salt and black pepper, to taste

Directions

1. Put the chicken thighs in a bowl and rub it with olive oil.

2. Take a bowl and mix paprika, salt, pepper, and garlic powder in it.

3. Rub the thighs with paprika, salt, pepper, and garlic powder.

4. Coat the things evenly from all the sides.

5. Put the chicken in the Instant Omni plus air fryer toaster oven basket and place it inside the air fryer for cooking.

6. Remember to put the chicken skin side down.

7.Fry for about 18 minutes, then flip the chicken piece and cook for more 10 minutes.

8.Once done, serve.

Nutrition Facts

Servings: 1

Amount per serving

Calories 773

% Daily Value*

Total Fat 54.2g 69%

Saturated Fat 14g 70%

Cholesterol 360mg 120%

Sodium 301mg 13%

Total Carbohydrate 2.7g 1%

Dietary Fiber 0.7g 3%

Total Sugars 0.8g

Protein 76.6g

Vitamin D 0mcg 0%

Calcium 59mg 5%

Iron 2mg 10%

Potassium 1136mg 2

24

CHICKEN WINGS IN AIR FRYER

These are the juiciest chicken wings recipe that you ever try. It is cooked within 20 minutes and gives mouthwatering taste and flavors.

Preparation Time: 10 Minutes
Cooking Time: 30-60 Minutes
Yield: 5- 6Servings
Ingredients

- 2 pounds chicken wing sections
- 1 tablespoon olive oil
- Salt and black pepper, to taste
- 1 cup hot sauce
- Oil sprays, for greasing

Directions

1.Wash and pat dry the chicken wings.

2.In a medium bowl, combine the chicken wings, oil, salt, and black pepper.

3.Spray the air fryer basket with cooking spray.

4.Layer the wings in a single layer on the Instant Omni plus air fryer toaster oven basket.

5.According to capacity cook the wings in batches.

6.Cook the chicken wings on 400 degrees F for 10 minutes and then flip.

7.Continue cooking for 15 more minutes until the skin is crispy.

8.Repeat for all batches.

9.Serve with hot sauce.

Nutrition Facts

Servings: 6

Amount per serving

Calories 510

% Daily Value*

Total Fat 36.1g 46%

Saturated Fat 9.5g 48%

Cholesterol 122mg 41%

Sodium 1131mg 49%

Total Carbohydrate 4.3g 2%

Dietary Fiber 0.3g 1%

Total Sugars 0.5g

Protein 39.7g

Vitamin D 0mcg 0%

Calcium 26mg 2%

Iron 2mg 12%

Potassium 323mg 7%

25

OMNI AIR FRYER CRISPY CHICKEN WINGS

It is a very simple yet easiest swing recipe you ever try.

Preparation Time: 20 Minutes

Cooking Time: 30-60 Minutes

Yield: 4 Servings

Ingredients

- 12 Chicken Wings
- 2 tablespoons of all seasoning rub
- 1/4 cup melted butter

Directions

1. Wash and pat dry the wings with a paper towel.

2. Put the dripping pan on the lower chamber/rack of the air fryer.

3. Melt butter in the microwave for 1 minute.

4. Baste the wings with butter and season it with salt and pepper, and all seasoning rub.

5. Put the wings in the Instant Omni plus air fryer toaster oven basket.

6. Put the basket on the top rack.

7. Adjust the temperature to 400 degrees F, set the time to 30 minutes, and touch the START.

8.Flip each wing after 15 minutes of cooking.

9.Cook the wings in batches according to capacity.

10. Once the wings get crispy and golden brown from outside, take out and serve.

Nutrition Facts

Servings: 4

Amount per serving

Calories 934

% Daily Value*

Total Fat 44g 56%

Saturated Fat 16.2g 81%

Cholesterol 420mg 140%

Sodium 458mg 20%

Total Carbohydrate 0g 0%

Dietary Fiber 0g 0%

Total Sugars 0g

Protein 126.8g

Vitamin D 8mcg 40%

Calcium 69mg 5%

Iron 5mg 29%

Potassium 1068mg 23%

26

BALSAMIC VINEGAR CHICKEN BREASTS

Here is the recipe that makes it easy to prepare some delicious roasted chicken in a lesser amount of time.

Preparation Time: 15 Minutes

Cooking Time: 30 20 Minutes

Yield: 4 Servings

Ingredients

- 6 tablespoons of coconut oil
- 1/4 cup balsamic vinegar
- 4 cloves garlic, minced
- 1/2 teaspoon of ginger, grated
- 1 tablespoon of basil, fresh
- Salt and black pepper, to taste
- 1.5 pounds chicken breasts, boneless and skinless

Directions

1.Take a bowl and mix coconut oil, garlic, ginger, salt, black pepper, and basil along with balsamic vinegar.

2.Marinate chicken in it for 2 hours.

3.Remember to evenly coat the chicken with the mixture.

4.Take out the chicken 30 minutes before cooking.

5.Now transfer the chicken to a baking pan and place it inside the Instant Omni plus air fryer toaster oven.

6.Set a timer to 30 minutes at 400 degrees F.

7.Remember to flip the chicken halfway through.

8.Once it's done serve.

Nutrition Facts

Servings: 4

Amount per serving

Calories 508

% Daily Value*

Total Fat 33g 42%

Saturated Fat 21.1g 106%

Cholesterol 151mg 50%

Sodium 148mg 6%

Total Carbohydrate 1.3g 0%

Dietary Fiber 0.1g 0%

Total Sugars 0.1g

Protein 49.4g

Vitamin D 0mcg 0%

Calcium 34mg 3%

Iron 2mg 12%

Potassium 442mg 9%

27

CLASSIC CHICKEN THIGHS

The richness of mustard gives this recipe a unique taste and flavor.

Preparation Time: 10 Minutes
Cooking Time: 25 Minutes
Yield: 2 Servings
Ingredients
- 6 chicken thighs
- 1 tablespoon coconut oil
- 1 teaspoon dry mustard
- 1/4 teaspoon thyme
- 1/4 teaspoon garlic powder
- 1/4 teaspoon dried marjoram
- Salt and freshly ground black pepper, to taste

Directions

1.Take a bowl and mix coconut oil, dry mustard, thyme, garlic powder, marjoram, salt, and black pepper.

2.Drench the thighs into the bowl mixture and rub for fine coating.

3.Place the thighs in the Instant Omni plus air fryer toaster oven basket and roast for 25 minutes.

4.Once cooked, serve hot.

Nutrition Facts

Servings: 2

Amount per serving

Calories 900

% Daily Value*

Total Fat 39.8g 51%

Saturated Fat 14.8g 74%

Cholesterol 390mg 130%

Sodium 377mg 16%

Total Carbohydrate 1g 0%

Dietary Fiber 0.4g 1%

Total Sugars 0.2g

Protein 127.2g

Vitamin D 0mcg 0%

Calcium 79mg 6%

Iron 6mg 32%

Potassium 1082mg 23%

28

CHICKEN WINGS WITH SESAME AND SOY SAUCE

The addition of sesame seeds makes it rich in protein.

Preparation Time: 15 Minutes

Cooking Time: 25minutes

Yield: 2 Servings

Ingredients

- 2 tablespoons of sesame seeds
- 2 tablespoons of olive oil
- 2 tablespoons of honey
- 1 tablespoon of soy sauce
- 1/2 tablespoon of ginger garlic paste
- 8 chicken drumsticks

Directions

1.Place the first five ingredients in a plastic zip-lock bag.

2.Put chicken drumsticks in it.

3.Marinate it in the refrigerator for 2.

4.Takeout 20 minutes before cooking hours.

5.Put the dumb stick-on the air fryer baking tray.

6.The marinated drumsticks in the basket of the fryer.

7.Cook for 25-30 minutes at 400 degrees F.

8.Once the chicken is crispy golden outside and crispy inside, serve.

Nutrition Facts

Servings: 2

Amount per serving

Calories 551

% Daily Value*

Total Fat 29g 37%

Saturated Fat 5.4g 27%

Cholesterol 162mg 54%

Sodium 600mg 26%

Total Carbohydrate 20g 7%

Dietary Fiber 1.2g 4%

Total Sugars 17.4g

Protein 52.8g

Vitamin D 0mcg 0%

Calcium 111mg 9%

Iron 4mg 23%

Potassium 437mg 9%

29

AIR FRYER CHICKEN BREASTS

This chicken breast recipe can be seasoned with your favorite season and cook for about 30 minutes using an Omni air fryer toaster oven.

Preparation Time: 10 Minutes

Cooking Time: 27-30 Minutes

Yield: 2 Servings

Ingredients

- 4 Chicken Breasts
- 3 tablespoons olive oil
- 3 tablespoons Creole Seasoning

Directions

1. Oil sprays the Instant Omni plus air fryer toaster oven basket.

2. Brush olive oil all over the breast pieces.

3. Season it with Creole seasoning.

4. Rub the season evenly on all the sides.

5. Put the breasts into the basket; try to keep a good space between each for pieces.

6. Place basket into the air fryer and cook at 400 for 15 minutes.

7.Remove the basket and flip chicken breasts.

8.Cook for 10-12 more minutes.

9.Once done, serve.

Nutrition Facts

Servings: 2

Amount per serving

Calories 735

% Daily Value*

Total Fat 42.6g 55%

Saturated Fat 9g 45%

Cholesterol 260mg 87%

Sodium 5111mg 222%

Total Carbohydrate 0g 0%

Dietary Fiber 0g 0%

Total Sugars 0g

Protein 84.5g

Vitamin D 0mcg 0%

Calcium 44mg 3%

Iron 4mg 20%

Potassium 710mg 15%

30

TERIYAKI CHICKEN BREASTS

It is a perfect tasting recipe rich in minerals, vitamins, and protein.

Preparation Time: 10 Minutes

Cooking Time: 20 Minutes

Yield: 2 Servings

Ingredients

- 4 Chicken Breasts, diced
- 3/4 cup soy sauce
- 2/3 cup sugar
- 2 slices lemon
- 3 cloves garlic, minced
- 1 teaspoon grated ginger

Directions

1. Take a skillet and pour soy sauce, sugar, lemon, ginger, and garlic in it.

2. Bring to a boil.

3. Then add chicken to it and coat the chicken well with the mixture, turn off the heat.

4. Oil sprays the baking pan.

5. Now layer the chicken in the Instant Omni plus air fryer toaster oven baking sheet.

6.Set temperature to 400 degrees F, and cook the chicken for 8 minutes.

7.Turn the chicken pieces and then cook or 8 more minutes.

8.Once done, serve.

Nutrition Facts

Servings: 2

Amount per serving

Calories 543

% Daily Value*

Total Fat 1.3g 2%

Saturated Fat 0.4g 2%

Cholesterol 105mg 35%

Sodium 8566mg 372%

Total Carbohydrate 83.1g 30%

Dietary Fiber 1.2g 4%

Total Sugars 68.9g

Protein 55.5g

Vitamin D 0mcg 0%

Calcium 47mg 4%

Iron 3mg 17%

Potassium 443mg 9%

RED MEAT RECIPES

31

AIR FRYER BACON CAULIFLOWER WITH CHEESE

Preparation Time: 20 Minutes

Cooking Time: 15 Minutes

Yield: 4 Servings

Ingredients

- 6 strips bacon
- 1cup cooked red meat, grounded
- 1 cup of water
- 1 medium cauliflower diced small
- 6 ounces cream cheese
- 1/3 cup heavy cream
- 2.5 cups shredded cheddar cheese
- Salt, to taste
- 1/4 teaspoon cayenne pepper
- 2 teaspoons paprika

Directions

1.Layer the air fryer baking tray with bacon and cooked it at 390 degrees F, for 5 minutes.

2.Put cauliflower in a bowl and pour in one cup of water.

3.Microwave it for 5 minutes until the cauliflower gets tender.

4.Take out and drain the cauliflower.

5.Put the cauliflower in a small bowl, and combine cheddar cheese, cream cheese, heavy cream, salt, cayenne pepper, cooked bacon, grounded meat, and paprika.

6.Mix the ingredients well and then transfer this mixture into an Instant Omni plus air fryer toaster oven baking dish.

7.Cook it in Omni air fryer for 5 minutes.

8.Once done serve and enjoy.

Nutrition Facts

Servings: 4

Amount per serving

Calories 828

% Daily Value*

Total Fat 71.1g 91%

Saturated Fat 36.5g 182%

Cholesterol 191mg 64%

Sodium 1941mg 84%

Total Carbohydrate 9g 3%

Dietary Fiber 1.7g 6%

Total Sugars 3.8g

Protein 38.7g

Vitamin D 14mcg 68%

Calcium 606mg 47%

Iron 2mg 12%

Potassium 467mg 10%

32

AIR FRYER ROAST BEEF

It is cooked within 20 minutes and gives mouthwatering taste and flavors.

Preparation Time: 20 Minutes
Cooking Time: 20 Minutes
Yield: 4 Servings
Ingredients

- 2 pounds beef roast
- 1 tablespoon olive oil
- 1 teaspoon onion powder
- Salt & pepper
- 2 teaspoons of rosemary
- 1 cup roasted vegetables

Directions

1.Wash and pat dry the roast with a paper towel.

2.Sprinkle the roast with seasonings and olive oil.

3.Put the beef roast on a baking tray and transfer it to an Instant Omni plus air fryer toaster oven.

4.Cooked beef roast for 20 minutes at 350 degrees Fahrenheit.

5.Once the internal temperature is between 145 to 150, the meat is cooked in medium-well.

6.If you want the meat to be cooked in the medium then the internal temperature should be 135 degrees Fahrenheit.

7.Once cooked allow it to sit on the cooling rack for 10 minutes before serving.

8.Serve the meat with your favorite roasted vegetables.

Nutrition Facts

Servings: 4

Amount per serving

Calories 455

% Daily Value*

Total Fat 17.7g 23%

Saturated Fat 5.9g 29%

Cholesterol 203mg 68%

Sodium 150mg 7%

Total Carbohydrate 0.9g 0%

Dietary Fiber 0.3g 1%

Total Sugars 0.2g

Protein 68.9g

Vitamin D 0mcg 0%

Calcium 13mg 1%

Iron 43mg 238%

Potassium 925mg 20%

33

AIR FRYER REUBEN ROLL-UPS

It is a very mouthwatering treat to enjoy with less time to prepare.

Preparation Time: 20 Minutes

Cooking Time: 12 Minutes

Yield: 4 Servings

Ingredients

- 2 packages of refrigerated crescent rolls
- 14 slices of Smoked Meat
- 10 slices of Swiss cheese
- 8 ounces of Sauerkraut
- Bagel seasoning, as needed
- Thousand Island dressing, as needed

Directions

1. The First Step is to enroll the Crescent dough and put it on a flat surface and separate it into 8 rectangles.

2. Cut the cheese slices in half and place it onto the rectangle shapes.

3. Put two slices of meat on top of each cheese slice.

4. End it with the topping of sauerkraut.

5. Roll up into style of the jelly roll and pinch to seal.

6.Cut each roll in half and place it on the cooking sheet that is lined with parchment paper.

7.Sprinkle the Bagel seasoning on top.

8.Cook it at 350 degrees Fahrenheit for 12 minutes in the Instant Omni plus air fryer toaster oven.

9.Once done, serve it with the Thousand Island dressing.

Nutrition Facts

Servings: 4

Amount per serving

Calories 765

% Daily Value*

Total Fat 44.6g 57%

Saturated Fat 13.9g 70%

Cholesterol 65mg 22%

Sodium 654mg 28%

Total Carbohydrate 12.3g 4%

Dietary Fiber 1.7g 6%

Total Sugars 3.5g

Protein 75.9g

Vitamin D 31mcg 154%

Calcium 571mg 44%

Iron 1mg 8%

Potassium 220mg 5%

34

ROAST BEEF

This beef recipe is cooked to its perfection using instant pot Omni air fryer oven

Preparation Time: 10 Minutes

Cooking Time: 30 Minutes

Yield: 4 Servings

Ingredients

- 2 pounds Beef Roast (can go up to 4 pounds)
- 1 tablespoon Olive Oil
- 2 tablespoons of Montreal Steak seasoning
- Oil spray, for greasing

Directions

1. Rub the roast meat with olive oil.

2. Season it with Montreal steak seasoning.

3. Take a baking tray and grease it with oil spray.

4. You can also use rotisserie of air fryer to cook the beef.

5. Now put the roast on an Instant Omni plus air fryer toaster oven baking tray, and bake it in the air fryer at 360 degrees F, for 15 -minutes per pound for medium-rare.

6. Allow rest for 5 minutes before serving.

Tips

1. The following temperatures for beef should be used
2. Rare: 115 to 120°F (125 final temperatures)
3. Medium-Rare: 125 to 130°F (135 final temperatures)
4. Medium-Well: 140 to 145°F (150 final temperatures)
5. Medium: 135 to 140°F
6. (145 final temperature)
7. Well-Done: 150 to 155°F (160 final temperatures)

Nutrition Facts

Servings: 4

Amount per serving

Calories 453

% Daily Value*

Total Fat 17.8g 23%

Saturated Fat 5.9g 29%

Cholesterol 203mg 68%

Sodium 149mg 6%

Total Carbohydrate 0g 0%

Dietary Fiber 0g 0%

Total Sugars 0g

Protein 68.8g

Vitamin D 0mcg 0%

Calcium 3mg 0%

Iron 43mg 237%

Potassium 913mg 19%

35

DIJON ROSEMARY BURGER PATTIES

These are quick and healthy patties to make any time at home.

Preparation Time: 10 Minutes

Cooking Time: 18-20 Minutes

Yield: 2 Servings

Ingredients

Burger Mixture

- 1 pound ground beef
- 1/4 cup Panko breadcrumbs
- 1/4 cup onion finely chopped
- 3 tablespoons Dijon mustard
- 3 teaspoons soy sauce
- 2 teaspoons fresh rosemary finely chopped
- Salt, to taste

Sauce Mixture Ingredients

- 2 teaspoons Dijon mustard
- 1 tablespoon brown sugar
- 1 teaspoon of soy sauce

Serving Ingredients (Toppings)

- 2 Toasted burger buns
- Favorite burger toppings

Directions

1.Take a large bowl, and mix all the burger mixture ingredients.

2.Make patties with hands.

3.Now, put a dripping pan on the lower rack of the air fryer Omni oven.

4.Take a separate bowl, and mix all sauce ingredients in it.

5.Put the patties on the Instant Omni plus air fryer toaster oven rack.

6.Select AIRFRY, and then adjust the temperature to 370 degrees F.

7.Set timer to 15 minutes, then touch the start button.

8.Once the timer completes, brush the patties with sauce.

9.Turn on the broil button, and set the timer to 3 minutes and start.

10. When the Broil program is complete, remove the patties.

11. Serve hot on toasted buns with favorite toppings.

Nutrition Facts

Servings: 2

Amount per serving

Calories 748

% Daily Value*

Total Fat 22g 28%

Saturated Fat 10g 50%

Cholesterol 202mg 67%

Sodium 1433mg 62%

Total Carbohydrate 55.7g 20%

Dietary Fiber 5.3g 19%

Total Sugars 9.2g

Protein 77.6g

Vitamin D 0mcg 0%

Calcium 143mg 11%

Iron 11mg 63%

Potassium 1163mg 25%

36

BEEF PATTIES

It is a mouthwatering patties recipe, that using some aromatic herb and spices.

Preparation Time: 15 Minutes
Cooking Time: 25 Minutes
Yield: 4 Servings
Ingredients
- 2 pounds of beef, boneless and grounded
- Grounded black pepper, to taste
- Salt, to taste
- 1 white onion, chopped
- 2 green peppers, chopped
- 1/2 teaspoon coriander powder
- 1/2 teaspoon of turmeric
- 1/2 teaspoon of cumin, ground
- 1 egg, cooked
- Oil spray, olive oil

Directions
1. Take a bowl and combine all the ingredients in it.
2. Make patties with hand.
3. Oil sprays the Patties from both sides.

4.Arrange in Instant Omni plus air fryer toaster oven pan or cooking sheet.

5.Cook at 370 degrees for 25 minutes.

6.Flip after 15 minutes of cooking.

7.Serve hot.

Nutrition Facts

Servings: 4

Amount per serving

Calories 463

% Daily Value*

Total Fat 15.6g 20%

Saturated Fat 5.7g 29%

Cholesterol 244mg 81%

Sodium 207mg 9%

Total Carbohydrate 5.7g 2%

Dietary Fiber 1.7g 6%

Total Sugars 2.7g

Protein 71.1g

Vitamin D 4mcg 19%

Calcium 24mg 2%

Iron 43mg 241%

Potassium 1084mg 23%

37

LAMB CHOPS WITH YOGURT

It is a perfectly cooked lamb that is tender to perfections.

Preparation Time: 10 Minutes

Cooking Time: 15 Minutes

Yield: 2 Servings

Ingredients

- 4 tablespoons of low-fat yogurt, side serving
- 1 teaspoon of cumin seeds
- 1 tablespoon of coriander seeds, crushed
- 1/3 teaspoon chili powder
- 1 teaspoon Gram Masala
- 2 tablespoons lemon juice
- 1 teaspoon salt
- 4-6 lamb chops
- Oil spray, for greasing

Directions

1.Mix yogurt, cumin seeds, coriander seeds, chili powder, Garam Masala, lemon juice, and salt in a bowl.

2.Marinate the chops in it for few hours.

3.Now grease a Instant Omni plus air fryer toaster oven

baking sheet with foil and put a pork chop in it with space in between the chops.

4.Air fryer at 400 degrees for 15 minutes.

5.Serve and enjoy.

Nutrition Facts

Servings: 2

Amount per serving

Calories 1250

% Daily Value*

Total Fat 49g 63%

Saturated Fat 17.6g 88%

Cholesterol 590mg 197%

Sodium 1691mg 74%

Total Carbohydrate 3.2g 1%

Dietary Fiber 0.3g 1%

Total Sugars 2.5g

Protein 185.8g

Vitamin D 0mcg 0%

Calcium 154mg 12%

Iron 16mg 89%

Potassium 2311mg 49%

38

AIR FRYER PORK CHOPS

These are the juiciest pork chop recipe that you can enjoy and this won't need much time to prepare.

Preparation Time: 10 Minutes

Cooking Time: 20 Minutes

Yield: 2 Servings

Ingredients

- 4 boneless pork chops
- 2 tablespoons of pork rub
- 2 tablespoons olive oil
- Oil spray, for greasing
- 1 cup of coleslaw, fresh

Directions

1. Rub the pork chop with olive oil and season it with pork rub.

2. Put it on a cooling rack that is greased with oil spray.

3. Cook the pork chop for 20 minutes, at 400 degrees F, inside Instant Omni plus air fryer toaster oven.

4. Remember to flip the pork chops after 7 minutes of cooking.

5. Once done, let it rest for 5 minutes, then serve it with coleslaw.

Nutrition Facts

Servings: 2
Amount per serving
Calories 660
% Daily Value*
Total Fat 47.6g 61%
Saturated Fat 13.1g 66%
Cholesterol 113mg 38%
Sodium 1058mg 46%
Total Carbohydrate 10.5g 4%
Dietary Fiber 0g 0%
Total Sugars 0g
Protein 51g
Vitamin D 0mcg 0%
Calcium 22mg 2%
Iron 0mg 3%
Potassium 118mg 3%

39

INSTANT OMNI/OMNI PLUS BEEF KEBABS

These kebabs are simple, yet great in flavor which makes them a family hit.

Preparation Time: 20 Minutes
Cooking Time: 15 Minutes
Yield: 2 Servings
Ingredients
- 1/4 cup Olive Oil
- 1/4 cup Soy Sauce
- 1 tablespoon White Wine Vinegar
- 1 tablespoon Worcestershire Sauce
- 1 teaspoon Honey
- 1 tablespoon Garlic Seasoning

Beef Kebab Ingredients
- 2 pounds New York strip steak boneless
- 1 red onion cut in chunks
- 1 red pepper cut in chunks
- 1 green pepper cut in chunks
- Salt and black pepper, to taste

Directions

1.Take a bowl and mix olive oil, soy sauce, vinegar, Worcestershire sauce, honey, and garlic seasoning.

2.Mix well and then cut the steak into 1-inch pieces.

3.Marinade the beef pieces in prepares sauce for 2 hours in the refrigerator.

4.When ready for cooking take them out from the refrigerator and then cut the onions, red and green pepper.

5.Assemble the kebabs by skewering vegetables and cubes of steak on the skewer's accessory that comes with an air fryer.

6.Thread the Rotisserie Spit that came with the oven through the holes in the Carousel.

7.Make sure the metal piece insert the screws, are outward.

8.Insert the ends of the skewers into the holes on the carousel.

9.Place the Kebab Accessory into the Instant Omni plus air fryer toaster oven.

10. Close the door and turn on the "ROAST".

11. Set the Temperature to 400 degrees F for 15 minutes.

12. Once the cooking process is done, Take out the kebabs and serve with a sprinkle of salt and black pepper.

Nutrition Facts

Servings: 2

Amount per serving

Calories 827

% Daily Value*

Total Fat 38.5g 49%

Saturated Fat 8.1g 41%

Cholesterol 235mg 78%

Sodium 2002mg 87%

Total Carbohydrate 19.6g 7%

Dietary Fiber 2.7g 10%

Total Sugars 11.3g

Protein 98.2g

Vitamin D 0mcg 0%

Calcium 38mg 3%

Iron 10mg 55%

Potassium 1187mg 25%

40

PRIME RIBS

These are fully flavor ribs that you can make easy. The spices that we add in this recipe make it a mouthwatering recipe to enjoy.

Preparation time: 20 minutes

Cooking Time: 55 Minutes

Yield: 2 Servings

Ingredients

- 2 pounds prime Ribs
- 1 cup of BBQ Sauce
- 1 teaspoon of Parsley
- 1 tabelspoon Paprika
- 1 tablespon Onion Powder
- Salt and black pepper, to taste
- 3/4 Cup of Light Brown Sugar
- 1 cup Water
- 1 tablespoon of Apple Cider Vinegar
- 1 tablespoon Worcestershire sauce

Directions

1. Wash the ribs and remove e any membranes.
2. Pat dry the rib with a paper towel.

3.Make a spice rub by adding all the listed ingredients excluding ribs in a bowl.

4.Coat the ribs with the rub.

5.Put one of the Rotisserie Forks on one end of the Spit.

6.Insert it lengthwise, through the Roast and push onto the Fork.

7.Attach the other Fork to the other end.

8.Place foil on the bottom of Instant Omni plus air fryer toaster oven to collect any dripping.

9.Press "ROAST" and set the temperature to 450° F for 15 minutes.

10. After 15 minutes reduce temperature to 250° F and cook for 40 minutes.

11. Once done , serve and enjoy.

Nutrition Facts

Servings: 2

Amount per serving

Calories 816

% Daily Value*

Total Fat 35g 45%

Saturated Fat 8.5g 43%

Cholesterol 75mg 25%

Sodium 1257mg 55%

Total Carbohydrate 96.9g 35%

Dietary Fiber 4g 14%

Total Sugars 59.3g

Protein 28.1g

Vitamin D 0mcg 0%

Calcium 49mg 4%

Iron 0mg 2%

Potassium 80mg 2%

41

AIR FRYER CUBAN PORK CHUNKS

The meat that is cooked using air fryer takes less time and cook in a much healthier way with

Great flavor and texture.

Preparation Time: 15 Minutes

Cooking Time: 10 Minutes

Yield: 4 Servings

Ingredients

Marinade Ingredients

- 2-1/2 pounds Country Style Pork Ribs, boneless
- 1 cup Mojo
- 1 Onion sliced
- 4 cloves Garlic minced

Seasoning for Air Frying

- 2 tablespoons Olive Oil
- 1/2 teaspoon of Salt
- 1 Lime, juiced

Directions

1.Cut the pork into 2-inch chunks.

2.Slice onions, garlic and add to a zip lock bag along with mojo.

3.Let it sit for a few hours.

4.Preheat the Instant Omni plus air fryer toaster oven at 450 degrees F.

5.Take out the pork along with onion and ham slices.

6.Now gently coat the pork pieces with lime, oil, and salt.

7.Put the pork pieces into the air fryer basket.

8.Air Fry at 450 degrees F for 10 minutes.

9.Once done, serve.

Nutrition Facts

Servings: 4

Amount per serving

Calories 591

% Daily Value*

Total Fat 39.6g 51%

Saturated Fat 12.3g 61%

Cholesterol 213mg 71%

Sodium 467mg 20%

Total Carbohydrate 1g 0%

Dietary Fiber 0.1g 0%

Total Sugars 0g

Protein 55.4g

Vitamin D 0mcg 0%

Calcium 56mg 4%

Iron 3mg 15%

Potassium 12mg 0%

42

PORK TENDERLOIN

If you are meat lover, then this recipe serve you well.

Preparation Time: 10 Minutes

Cooking Time: 20 Minutes

Yield: 2 Servings

Ingredients

- 1 pound of pork tenderloin
- 2 tablespoons honey
- 2 tablespoons Sriracha hot sauce or to taste
- Salt, to taste

Directions

1. Screw the meat on a rotisserie skewer of Instant Omni plus air fryer toaster oven.

2. Combine the honey, Sriracha, and salt in a bowl and brush it on the meat.

3. Put the drip pan at the bottom of the cooking chamber.

4. Adjust the temperature to 350°F and set the time to 20 minutes, and then touch START.

5. Use the rotisserie fetch tool to lift the spit into the oven chamber.

6. Close the door and touch ROTATE.

7.Once the timer compete, serve

Nutrition Facts

Servings: 2

Amount per serving

Calories 388

% Daily Value*

Total Fat 8g 10%

Saturated Fat 2.7g 14%

Cholesterol 166mg 55%

Sodium 208mg 9%

Total Carbohydrate 17.3g 6%

Dietary Fiber 0g 0%

Total Sugars 17.3g

Protein 59.4g

Vitamin D 0mcg 0%

Calcium 15mg 1%

Iron 3mg 15%

Potassium 966mg 21%

43

AIR FRYER SAUSAGE AND PEPPERS

It is a quick and easy recipe that can be enjoyed as dinner or lunch.

Preparation Time: 10 Minutes

Cooking Time: 22 Minutes

Yield: 4 Servings

Ingredients

- 4 bell peppers red, sliced into strips
- 1/2 yellow onion sliced
- 1/2 green pepper, sliced
- 2 tablespoons olive oil
- Pinch sea salt and pepper
- 8 Italian meat sausages, pork or meat

Directions

1.Cut the slices of pepper and onion into the strip.

2.Season it with salt, black pepper and olive oil.

3.Place the ingredients in the air fryer basket.

4.Place sausages with pepper and onions in a baking tray.

5.Preheat the Instant Omni plus air fryer toaster oven to 400 degrees F.

6.Cook for 22 minutes, or until internal temperature reaches 160.

7.Take out and serve.

Nutrition Facts

Servings: 4

Amount per serving

Calories 631

% Daily Value*

Total Fat 52.3g 67%

Saturated Fat 16.8g 84%

Cholesterol 95mg 32%

Sodium 2004mg 87%

Total Carbohydrate 7.1g 3%

Dietary Fiber 0.2g 1%

Total Sugars 1.4g

Protein 31.7g

Vitamin D 0mcg 0%

Calcium 35mg 3%

Iron 2mg 13%

Potassium 505mg 11%

44

ORANGE AND HONEY BAKED HAM

Turn an ordinary ham into an extraordinary meat recipe, that gets its sweetness from the orange glazed.

Preparation Time: 10 Minutes
Cooking Time: 50 Minutes
Yield: 4 Servings
Ingredients
Glaze Ingredients
- 4 garlic cloves minced
- 4 teaspoons orange marmalade/jam
- 4 teaspoons Dijon mustard
- 3 tablespoons brown sugar
- 1 orange zest
- 1 cup Orange Juice
- 1 teaspoon of fresh rosemary
Ham Ingredients
- 2 pounds of fully cooked smoked ham
Directions
1.Take a mixing bowl and combine orange jam, mustard, sugar, zest, and juice.

2.Blend all ingredients in a blender.

3.Once the smooth glaze is formed take out in a bowl.

4.Set your Instant Omni plus air fryer toaster oven to bake function at 360°F for 50 minutes.

5.Place the ham on top of the oil greased baking pan and pour the glaze over top of the ham.

6.Cook until the the internal temperature reaches 145 degrees F.

7.Enjoy.

Nutrition Facts

Servings: 4

Amount per serving

Calories 450

% Daily Value*

Total Fat 19.8g 25%

Saturated Fat 6.7g 33%

Cholesterol 129mg 43%

Sodium 3021mg 131%

Total Carbohydrate 28.8g 10%

Dietary Fiber 3.3g 12%

Total Sugars 14.6g

Protein 37.9g

Vitamin D 0mcg 0%

Calcium 67mg 5%

Iron 3mg 14%

Potassium 670mg 14%

45

SLICED PINEAPPLE HAM STEAKS

It is a good way to enjoy any leftover ham. It can be served with boiled asparagus and sliced eggs.

Preparation Time: 10 Minutes

Cooking Time: 10 Minutes

Yield: 4 Servings

Ingredients

- 4 slices of pineapple
- 4 slices of ham, 1 inch thick
- 2 cherry tomatoes
- 4 sprigs fresh thyme
- 2 tablespoons orange marmalade
- 2 tablespoons butter, melted
- 2 teaspoons pineapple juice from the can
- 1 tablespoon lemon juice
- Salt and black pepper to taste

Side Serving

- 4 boiled eggs
- 1cup of asparagus, boiled

Directions

1.Put the ham slices on a baking sheet layered with parchment pepper.

2.Pour melted butter in a bowl and add pineapple juice, marmalade, lemon juice, and salt and black pepper

3.Mix it well.

4.Put this glaze onto the ham slices.

5.Lay the cherry tomato, thyme and pineapple rings on top of each ham.

6.Set the Instant Omni plus air fryer toaster oven to bake at 450 degrees F, for 10 minutes.

7.Serve with egg and asparagus.

Nutrition Facts

Servings: 4

Amount per serving

Calories 126

% Daily Value*

Total Fat 8.1g 10%

Saturated Fat 4.4g 22%

Cholesterol 97mg 32%

Sodium 82mg 4%

Total Carbohydrate 10.6g 4%

Dietary Fiber 1.5g 6%

Total Sugars 8.5g

Protein 4.2g

Vitamin D 12mcg 58%

Calcium 32mg 2%

Iron 1mg 7%

Potassium 253mg 5%

SEAFOOD RECIPES

46

AIR FRYER BAKED SHRIMP

It is a very easy shrimp recipe that is made in instant Omni air fryer.

Preparation Time: 6 Minutes
Cooking Time: 10 Minutes
Yield: 2 Servings
Ingredients
- 1 pound of large shrimp
- 8 tablespoons butter
- 1 teaspoon minced garlic, minced
- 1/4 cup white wine
- Salt and black pepper, to taste
- 1/2 teaspoon cayenne pepper
- 1/4 teaspoon paprika
- 1/2 teaspoon onion powder
- 1/2 cup of bread crumbs

Directions

1.Take a bowl and combine breadcrumbs and seasoning including salt, black pepper, cayenne pepper, paprika, and onion powder.

2.Melt butter in a microwave and then add white wine and garlic to it.

3.Remove it from the heat and add shrimp to the butter.

4.Then dump it to the breadcrumbs and coat well.

5.Transfer the shrimp to the baking dish and put inside Instant Omni plus air fryer toaster oven.

6.Air fry it at 350 degrees F, for 10 minutes.

7.Serve and enjoy!

Nutrition Facts

Servings: 2

Amount per serving

Calories 727

% Daily Value*

Total Fat 47.6g 61%

Saturated Fat 29.5g 148%

Cholesterol 446mg 149%

Sodium 811mg 35%

Total Carbohydrate 25.7g 9%

Dietary Fiber 1.5g 5%

Total Sugars 2.2g

Protein 46.9g

Vitamin D 32mcg 159%

Calcium 71mg 5%

Iron 2mg 9%

Potassium 123mg 3%

47

TASTY SHRIMP

It is a very simple, easy recipe that fits for two.

Preparation Time: 15 Minutes

Cooking Time: 12 Minutes

Yield: 2servings

Ingredients

- 1.5 pounds shrimps, peeled and deveined
- Oil spray, for greasing

Bread Crumb Ingredients

- 1 cup bread crumbs
- 1/2 tablespoon cumin
- 1/2 teaspoon paprika
- 1 teaspoon of lemon zest
- Sea salt, to taste

Ingredients for the Sauce

- 4 teaspoons of coconut oil
- 1/2 teaspoon of onion powder
- 2 teaspoons ginger, freshly grated
- 2 cloves garlic, minced
- 1 tablespoon of tomato paste
- 2 tablespoons red Thai curry paste

- 2l fat coconut milk
- Salt, to taste
- 1/2 cup cilantro for garnish

Directions

1.Combine all the listed sauce ingredients in a bowl and set aside for further use.

2.Mix all the bread crumb ingredients in a bowl and mix well.

3.Coat each shrimp with the sauce mixture and then dump it to bread crumbs to coat the shrimps well.

4.Repeat for all the shrimps.

5.Layer the shrimp on baking tray grease with oil spray.

6.Cook for 12 minutes at 390 degrees F, in Instant Omni plus air fryer toaster oven.

7.Once done, serve with prepared sauce.

Nutrition Facts

Servings: 2

Amount per serving

Calories 628

% Daily Value*

Total Fat 9.3g 12%

Saturated Fat 2.5g 12%

Cholesterol 716mg 239%

Sodium 1345mg 58%

Total Carbohydrate 45.2g 16%

Dietary Fiber 2.9g 10%

Total Sugars 3.5g

Protein 85.1g

Vitamin D 0mcg 0%

Calcium 422mg 32%

Iron 5mg 27%

Potassium 724mg 15%

48

CRUNCHY COD FILLET AND SLICED POTATOES

It is a weekend hit, tasty recipe of fish that is prepared with the twist of the addition of potatoes.

Preparation Time: 15 Minutes

Cooking Time: 15minutes

Yield: 2 Servings

Ingredients

- 3 russet potatoes, sliced
- 2 tablespoons of butter
- 4 cloves garlic
- Salt and black pepper, to taste
- 4 cod fillets
- 2 tablespoons olive oil

Side Serving

- 1/2 cup mayonnaise

Directions

1.Add butter, olive oil, garlic, salt, and pepper in a bowl.

2.And melt it in a microwave for a few minutes.

3.Now clean russet potatoes and slice potatoes use a mandolin slicer.

4.Brush garlic butter on the slices of potatoes.

5.Layer potatoes on the baking sheet, without overlapping.

6.Brush fish fillet with remaining butter.

7.Put the fish fillet on top of potato slice and cook in Instant Omni plus air fryer toaster oven for 15 minutes at 390 degrees F.

8.Then serve with mayonnaise.

Nutrition Facts

Servings: 2

Amount per serving

Calories 800

% Daily Value*

Total Fat 46g 59%

Saturated Fat 12.4g 62%

Cholesterol 61mg 20%

Sodium 960mg 42%

Total Carbohydrate 85.3g 31%

Dietary Fiber 8.8g 31%

Total Sugars 7.5g

Protein 16.4g

Vitamin D 8mcg 40%

Calcium 59mg 5%

Iron 3mg 16%

Potassium 1526mg 32%

49

FISH FILLET RECIPES FOR LUNCH

It is a very simple recipe that is rich in omega 3 and other essential nutrients.

Preparation Time: 20 Minutes

Cooking Time: 15 Minutes

Yield: 2 Servings

Ingredients

- 1 cup breadcrumbs
- Salt and black pepper, to taste
- 2 tablespoons fresh parsley
- 250 grams firm white fish fillet
- 1 cup plain all-purpose flour
- 4 organic eggs, whisked

Sauce Ingredients

- 1 cup mayonnaise
- 1 tablespoon of capers, drained
- 2 jalapeños, chopped
- 4 tablespoons of soy sauce
- 1/2 teaspoon of red chili flakes
- Salt, pinch
- 1/2 teaspoon of brown sugar

Directions

1.In a large bowl, add salt, pepper, parsley, and breadcrumbs.

2.In a separate small bowl, whisk all the sauce ingredients.

3.Cut fish in small bite-size pieces.

4.Whisk organic egg in a small separate bowl.

5.Now take a flat plate and place the flour in it.

6.Dip the fish pieces in the flour, then in whisked eggs, and then at the end in breadcrumbs.

7.Repeat once all the pieces are coated.

8.Place the fish in an Instant Omni plus air fryer toaster oven baking tray and cook for about 15 minutes at 375 degrees F.

9.Serve with the sauce.

10. Enjoy.

Nutrition Facts

Servings: 2

Amount per serving

Calories 1506

% Daily Value*

Total Fat 53.2g 68%

Saturated Fat 9.3g 46%

Cholesterol 358mg 119%

Sodium 3366mg 146%

Total Carbohydrate 210.7g 77%

Dietary Fiber 8.8g 32%

Total Sugars 13g

Protein 40.5g

Vitamin D 31mcg 154%

Calcium 185mg 14%

Iron 10mg 54%

Potassium 499mg 11%

50

LEMON GARLIC FISH

It is a very tangy and garlic fish recipe to enjoy.

Preparation Time: 14 Minutes

Cooking Time: 12 Minutes

Yield: 2 Servings

Ingredients

- 1 pound cod fish fillet, skinless
- 3 cloves of garlic, minced
- 1-Inch ginger, minced
- 3 small lemons, juice only
- 2 tablespoons olive oil
- Salt, to taste
- Black pepper, to taste
- 1/4 teaspoon of turmeric
- Oil spray, for coating

Directions

1. Take a bowl and combine garlic, ginger, olive oil, salt, pepper, lemon juice, and turmeric.

2. Coat the fish fillet with a generous amount of it.

3. Now layer the fish fillet in a baking dish that is a coat with oil spray.

4.Air fry it in Instant Omni plus air fryer toaster oven, at 390 degrees F, for 12 minutes.

5.Once done, serve and enjoy.

Nutrition Facts

Servings: 2

Amount per serving

Calories 368

% Daily Value*

Total Fat 16.3g 21%

Saturated Fat 2.4g 12%

Cholesterol 125mg 42%

Sodium 255mg 11%

Total Carbohydrate 1.7g 1%

Dietary Fiber 0.2g 1%

Total Sugars 0.1g

Protein 52.1g

Vitamin D 0mcg 0%

Calcium 41mg 3%

Iron 1mg 7%

Potassium 579mg 12%

51

ALASKAN COD WITH FENNEL AND OLIVES

It is a family hit recipe that is loved by all.

Preparation Time: 15 Minutes

Cooking Time: 12 Minutes

Yield: 2 Servings

Ingredients

- 4 tablespoons olive oil
- Salt and black pepper, to taste
- 1 garlic clove, minced
- 2 tablespoons of lemon juice
- 1 large tomato, sliced
- 1 cup green olives, pitted and crushed
- 1/2 head fennel, quartered
- 14 ounces Alaskan cod fillets, cut into 3-inch cube

Directions

1.Season the salmon with salt, garlic, black pepper, and lemon juice.

2.Coat it generously with olive oil.

3.Put in on to a baking tray and top it with fennels, green olives, and tomato slices.

4.Sprinkle salt and pepper on top and drizzle some olive oil.

5.Cook in the Instant Omni plus air fryer toaster oven for 12-17 minutes at 390 degrees.

6.Once done, serve.

Nutrition Facts

Servings: 2

Amount per serving

Calories 488

% Daily Value*

Total Fat 34.4g 44%

Saturated Fat 4.8g 24%

Cholesterol 70mg 23%

Sodium 833mg 36%

Total Carbohydrate 10.2g 4%

Dietary Fiber 3.7g 13%

Total Sugars 2.7g

Protein 37.2g

Vitamin D 0mcg 0%

Calcium 94mg 7%

Iron 3mg 16%

Potassium 338mg 7%

52

SHRIMP AND ASPARAGUS

The addition of vegetables like asparagus masks this recipe much healthier and filling.

Preparation Time: 20 Minutes

Cooking Time: 15 Minutes

Yield: 1-2 Servings

Ingredients

- 1 bunch asparagus
- Salt and black pepper, to taste
- 1 pound shrimp peeled and deveined
- 1 lemon, wedges
- 6 tablespoons of butter, melted

Directions

1.Take a bowl and add butter, salt, pepper, and lemon wedges.

2.Add shrimp and asparagus, toss to coat the ingredients well.

3.Put the ingredient in the Instant Omni plus air fryer toaster oven, baking sheet and bake it for 15 minutes at 390 degrees F, in Omni air fryer toaster oven.

4.Once done, serve.

Nutrition Facts

Servings: 2

Amount per serving

Calories 543

% Daily Value*

Total Fat 37.1g 48%

Saturated Fat 22.6g 113%

Cholesterol 534mg 178%

Sodium 755mg 33%

Total Carbohydrate 2.7g 1%

Dietary Fiber 1.4g 5%

Total Sugars 1.3g

Protein 49.3g

Vitamin D 24mcg 119%

Calcium 115mg 9%

Iron 8mg 47%

Potassium 559mg 12%

53

PANKO-CRUSTED COD

It is a very easy, crunchy, and well-flavored recipe to enjoy.

Preparation Time: 20 Minutes

Cooking Time: 18 Minutes

Yield: 4 Servings

Ingredients

- 1 cup Panko bread crumbs
- 2 tablespoons of olive oil
- 2 teaspoons of lemon zest
- Salt, to taste
- 1/2 cup light mayonnaise
- 2 teaspoons lemon juice
- 1/2 teaspoon of thyme
- 4 cod fillets, 6 oz each

Directions

1. Take a skillet and add bread crumb to it.

2. Cook the bread crumbs for 2 minutes and add oil, lemon zest, and salt.

3. Mix well and set aside for further use.

4. Take a bowl and mix mayonnaise, lemon juice, and thyme.

5. Put the mayonnaise mixture equally over the cod fillet.

6.Place the cod fillet on a baking sheet that is coated with oil spray.

7.Cook in the Instant Omni plus air fryer toaster oven at 390 for 15 minutes.

8.Take out and sprinkle bread crumb mixture on top.

9.Serve and enjoy.

Nutrition Facts

Servings: 4

Amount per serving

Calories 823

% Daily Value*

Total Fat 21.3g 27%

Saturated Fat 2.8g 14%

Cholesterol 218mg 73%

Sodium 956mg 42%

Total Carbohydrate 26.8g 10%

Dietary Fiber 1.3g 5%

Total Sugars 3.7g

Protein 135.9g

Vitamin D 0mcg 0%

Calcium 57mg 4%

Iron 2mg 9%

Potassium 63mg 1%

54

AIR FRYER HEALTHY WHITE FISH WITH GARLIC & LEMON

It is a very irresistible recipe to enjoy.

Preparation Time: 15 Minutes

Cooking Time: 10 Minutes

Yields: 2 Servings

Ingredients

- 12 ounces tilapia filets
- 2 tablespoons of olive oil
- 1/3 teaspoon garlic powder
- 1/3 teaspoon lemon pepper seasoning
- 1/3 teaspoon onion powder, optional
- Salt and black pepper, to taste

Directions

1. Wash and pat dry the fish fillet and coat it with a generous amount of olive oil.

2. Then season it with garlic powder, lemon pepper seasoning, onion powder, black pepper, and salt.

3. Place it on an Instant Omni plus air fryer toaster oven pan that is greased with oil spray.

4. Cook it for 10 minutes at 360 degrees Fahrenheit.

5. Check the fish with the Fork, if flaky the fish is done.

6.Serve.

Nutrition Facts

Servings: 2

Amount per serving

Calories 344

% Daily Value*

Total Fat 19g 24%

Saturated Fat 4g 20%

Cholesterol 100mg 33%

Sodium 661mg 29%

Total Carbohydrate 0.9g 0%

Dietary Fiber 0.2g 1%

Total Sugars 0.3g

Protein 44.2g

Vitamin D 0mcg 0%

Calcium 43mg 3%

Iron 2mg 9%

Potassium 653mg 14%

55

AIR FRYER SEAFOOD NOODLES

It is a very health recipe to enjoy as dinner.

Preparation Time: 15 Minutes

Cooking Time: 20 Minutes

Yields: 6 Servings

Ingredients

- 1.5 pounds of lasagna noodles
- Salt and black pepper, to taste
- 1/2 pound of shrimp, peeled and deveined, tails removed
- 1/2 pound Scallops
- 1/2 pound Crabmeat
- 1 cup Spaghetti sauce
- 1 cup Alfredo sauce
- Oregano, to taste
- 1 clove garlic minced
- 1 16 ounces of container ricotta
- 1/4 cup Parmesan
- 1 egg
- 1 cup Mozzarella cheese, grated
- 1 cup Mexican Cheese

Directions

1.Take a small bowl and mix salt, pepper, Alfredo sauce, oregano, garlic, spaghetti sauce.

2.Transfer it into a Skillet and cook for 5 minutes.

3.Take a large bowl, and add noodle and boiling water in it.

4.Cook the noodles in the water at medium flame.

5.Drain and set aside.

6.Now mix seafood with sauce.

7.In a separate small bowl, combine egg salt pepper parmesan. And ricotta.

8.Take another bowl and combine Mexican cheese and Mozzarella cheese.

9.Now take a Shallow baking tray and layer the bottom with the sauce.

10. Top it with noodles, then add ricotta mixture and end with cheese topping.

11. Put it in an Instant Omni plus air fryer toaster oven and cook for 20 minutes at 350 degrees Fahrenheit.

12. Let it sit for 10 minutes before serving.

Nutrition Facts

Servings: 6

Amount per serving

Calories 811

% Daily Value*

Total Fat 29.1g 37%

Saturated Fat 15.8g 79%

Cholesterol 231mg 77%

Sodium 2267mg 99%

Total Carbohydrate 87.4g 32%

Dietary Fiber 0.3g 1%

Total Sugars 2.9g

Protein 51.2g

Vitamin D 3mcg 13%

Calcium 630mg 48%

Iron 1mg 5%

Potassium 233mg 5%

56

SALMON AIR FRYER

It is a recipe rich in omega 3 and other nutrients.

Preparation Time: 15 Minutes

Cooking Time: 10 Minutes

Yields: 2 Servings

Ingredients

- 1 pound of smoked salmon
- 1 teaspoon of lemon juice
- 2 teaspoons of capers
- 1 egg small
- Salt and pepper, to taste
- 1/3 cup Panko Breadcrumbs

Sauce Ingredients

- 10 tablespoons mayonnaise
- 1 avocado, mashed

Directions

1.Shred the salmon into small pieces and put it in a large bowl.

2.Then add lemon juice, capers, eggs, salt, pepper, and Panko bread crumbs in a bowl.

3.Mix the ingredients and form small parties with the hand.

4.Flatten the patties and then put them into the baking tray.

5.Cook for 5 minutes at 350 degrees Fahrenheit in an Instant Omni plus air fryer toaster oven.

6.Flip to cook from the other side for 5 more minutes.

7.Meanwhile, take a bowl and mix all the sauce ingredients.

8.Once the patties are done, served with avocado Mayo sauce.

Nutrition Facts

Servings: 2

Amount per serving

Calories 809

% Daily Value*

Total Fat 54.4g 70%

Saturated Fat 9.9g 50%

Cholesterol 71mg 24%

Sodium 5231mg 227%

Total Carbohydrate 37.2g 14%

Dietary Fiber 8g 29%

Total Sugars 5.6g

Protein 45.6g

Vitamin D 0mcg 0%

Calcium 65mg 5%

Iron 3mg 17%

Potassium 893mg 19%

57

SWEET GARLIC SHRIMP

If you love sweet and salt together, then this recipe serves you well.

Preparation Time: 10 Minutes

Cooking Time: 15 Minutes

Yield: 2 Servings

Ingredients

- 1.5 pounds of shrimp, deveined

Sweet Garlic Sauce Ingredients

- 1/4 cup stevia
- 1/2 teaspoon of garlic, minced
- 1/2 teaspoon of ginger, minced
- 2 green onions, minced
- 4 tablespoons of olive oil
- Oil spray, for greasing
- Salt and black pepper, to taste

Directions

1. Take a bowl and mix salt, pepper, garlic, ginger, onions, olive oil, and stevia.

2. Now put the shrimp in this marinade and let it sit in the refrigerator for 2 hours.

3.Afterward, grease a baking tray with oil spray.

4.Put the shrimp and marinade on the baking tray.

5.Set a timer to 15 minutes at 390 degrees F inside an Instant Omni plus air fryer toaster oven.

6.Once done take out and serve.

Nutrition Facts

Servings: 2

Amount per serving

Calories 654

% Daily Value*

Total Fat 34.1g 44%

Saturated Fat 5.8g 29%

Cholesterol 716mg 239%

Sodium 833mg 36%

Total Carbohydrate 6.8g 2%

Dietary Fiber 0.5g 2%

Total Sugars 0.4g

Protein 77.8g

Vitamin D 0mcg 0%

Calcium 321mg 25%

Iron 1mg 8%

Potassium 627mg 13%

58

SEAFOOD BAKE FOR TWO

It is an easy, quick, and delicious way to make a seafood dinner time meal.

Preparation Time: 20 Minutes
Cooking Time: 15 Minutes
Yield: 2 Servings
Ingredients
- 2 halibut fillets, 4 ounces
- 2 scallops
- 2 jumbo shrimp, deveined
- 1/3 cup dry white wine
- 4 tablespoons melted butter
- 1/2 tablespoon lemon juice
- 1 teaspoon seafood seasoning, dry
- 1 teaspoon garlic, minced
- Salt and pepper, to taste

Directions
1. Take an air fryer baking dish and grease it with oil spray.
2. Add halibut, scallops, and shrimp in the baking dish and drizzle wine, lemon juice, and butter on top.
3. Season it with garlic, salt, pepper, and seafood seasoning.

4.Toss and then air fry it in Instant Omni plus air fryer toaster oven, for minutes at 390 degrees F.

5.Once it's done serve.

Nutrition Facts

Servings: 2

Amount per serving

Calories 664

% Daily Value*

Total Fat 31g 40%

Saturated Fat 15.5g 78%

Cholesterol 329mg 110%

Sodium 921mg 40%

Total Carbohydrate 2.4g 1%

Dietary Fiber 0.1g 0%

Total Sugars 0.4g

Protein 83.9g

Vitamin D 16mcg 80%

Calcium 74mg 6%

Iron 16mg 89%

Potassium 1460mg 31%

59

SALMON WITH PESTO

It is classic and elegant salmon recipes that offer some great taste and nutrition.

Preparation Time: 10 Minutes

Cooking Time: 12 Minutes

Yield: 2 Servings

Ingredients

- 1 pound salmon
- 1ounce green pesto
- Salt and black pepper, to taste
- 1 tablespoon of olive oil
- Oil spray, for greasing

Ingredients for Green Sauce

- 1 ounce of green pesto
- 1/3 cup mayonnaise
- 6 tablespoons Greek yogurt
- Salt and black pepper, to taste

Directions

1.Grease a baking sheet of the air fryer with oil spray.

2.Put the salmon skin-side down on the baking tray.

3.Season the salmon with salt and pepper.

4.Then coat it with olive oil.

5.Next, spread the pesto on top of the salmon.

6.Put the salmon on the baking sheet.

7.Bake the salmon in the Instant Omni plus air fryer toaster oven, at 390 degrees F, for about 12 minutes.

8.Stir the green sauce ingredients in a separate bowl.

9.Once salmon is cooked, serve it with sauces.

10. Enjoy.

Nutrition Facts

Servings: 2

Amount per serving

Calories 540

% Daily Value*

Total Fat 35g 45%

Saturated Fat 5.5g 27%

Cholesterol 112mg 37%

Sodium 389mg 17%

Total Carbohydrate 10.7g 4%

Dietary Fiber 0g 0%

Total Sugars 3.8g

Protein 47.7g

Vitamin D 0mcg 0%

Calcium 119mg 9%

Iron 2mg 9%

Potassium 922mg 20%

60

SALMON WITH BROCCOLI AND CHEESE

It is an aromatic, delicious, and easy seafood recipe that is prepared in 15 minutes.

Preparation Time: 15 Minutes

Cooking Time: 19 Minutes

Yield: 2 Servings

Ingredients

- 1 cup of broccoli florets
- 1/3 cup of butter, melted
- Salt and pepper, to taste
- 1/2 cup of grated cheddar cheese
- 1 pound of salmon fillet
- Water, as needed

Directions

1.Boil water in a cooking pot and add salt.

2.Simmer the broccoli in salted water for 5 minutes.

3.Drain the broccoli and place it on a paper towel.

4.Season salmon with salt and pepper.

5.Brush butter ob the salmon fillet.

6.Put the fillet on baking tray /sheet.

7.Top the fillet with cheese.

8. Put the broccoli on side of the salmon.

9. Bake it in the Instant Omni plus air fryer toaster oven for 12 minutes at 380 degrees F.

10. Broil for 2 minutes in the end.

11. Once it's done serve.

Nutrition Facts

Servings: 2

Amount per serving

Calories 701

% Daily Value*

Total Fat 54.2g 69%

Saturated Fat 27.4g 137%

Cholesterol 211mg 70%

Sodium 508mg 22%

Total Carbohydrate 3.4g 1%

Dietary Fiber 1.2g 4%

Total Sugars 0.9g

Protein 52.6g

Vitamin D 25mcg 123%

Calcium 314mg 24%

Iron 2mg 11%

Potassium 1052mg 22%

VEGAN & VEGETARIAN RECIPES

61

ROASTED VEGETABLES

The roasted vegetables can be cooked easily using air fryer Omni oven and toaster.

Preparation Time: 10 Minutes

Cooking Time: 20 Minutes

Yield: 4 Servings

Ingredients

- 1 cup broccoli, florets
- 1 cup cauliflower, florets
- 1 cup carrots, peeled and cubed
- 1 tablespoon coconut oil
- Oil spray, for greasing

Directions

1.Take a bowl and add all the listed vegetables in it.

2.Add coconut oil and toss the ingredients well for fine combination.

3.Transfer the vegetables into the baking tray, which is greased with oil spray.

4.Set the temperature to 380 degrees Fahrenheit, and cook the vegetables for 20 minutes , inside Instant Omni plus air fryer toaster oven.

5.Once golden brown takes out the vegetables from the tray and stir them and serve.

Nutrition Facts

Servings: 4

Amount per serving

Calories 56

% Daily Value*

Total Fat 3.7g 5%

Saturated Fat 3g 15%

Cholesterol 0mg 0%

Sodium 34mg 1%

Total Carbohydrate 5.5g 2%

Dietary Fiber 1.9g 7%

Total Sugars 2.3g

Protein 1.4g

Vitamin D 0mcg 0%

Calcium 25mg 2%

Iron 0mg 2%

Potassium 236mg 5%

62

VEGGIE FRITTERS

If you want to enjoy some fresh green beans and carrots that are air fry to its perfection then this healthy and colorful recipe is for you.

Preparation Time: 10 Minutes

Cooking Time: 10 Minutes

Yield: 3 Servings

Ingredients

- 1/2 pound green beans trimmed
- 1/2 pound carrots cut into sticks
- Salt and black pepper, to taste

Directions

1. Take a bowl and combine all the listed ingredients.

2. Toss well and load the vegetables into the cooking tray.

3. Cook at 400 degrees Fahrenheit for 10 minutes in the Instant Omni plus air fryer toaster oven.

4. Once done serve and enjoy with ranch.

Nutrition Facts

Servings: 3

Amount per serving

Calories 55

% Daily Value*
Total Fat 0.1g 0%
Saturated Fat 0g 0%
Cholesterol 0mg 0%
Sodium 57mg 2%
Total Carbohydrate 12.9g 5%
Dietary Fiber 4.4g 16%
Total Sugars 4.8g
Protein 2g
Vitamin D 0mcg 0%
Calcium 53mg 4%
Iron 1mg 6%
Potassium 400mg 9%

63

ASPARAGUS

It is the perfectly roasted asparagus recipe that is prepared in instant Omni air fryer toaster oven.

Preparation Time: 10 Minutes

Cooking Time: 6 Minutes

Yield: 2 Servings

Ingredients

- 1 pound of fresh asparagus
- 2 teaspoons extra virgin olive oil
- Salt and black pepper, to taste

Directions

1. Oil grease an Omni baking tray, and set aside for further use.

2. Take a bowl, and toss together asparagus, salt, black pepper, and olive oil.

3. Transfer vegetables into the baking tray of Instant Omni plus air fryer toaster oven.

4. Cook for 6 minutes at 400 degrees Fahrenheit.

5. Remember to toss the asparagus halfway through.

6. Once it's done remove from oven and serve.

Nutrition Facts

Servings: 2
Amount per serving
Calories 85
% Daily Value*
Total Fat 4.9g 6%
Saturated Fat 0.8g 4%
Cholesterol 0mg 0%
Sodium 5mg 0%
Total Carbohydrate 8.8g 3%
Dietary Fiber 4.8g 17%
Total Sugars 4.3g
Protein 5g
Vitamin D 0mcg 0%
Calcium 55mg 4%
Iron 5mg 27%
Potassium 459mg 10%

64

GARLIC PARMESAN BROCCOLI

If you want to add some vegetables to your diet then this crispy caramelized broccoli that has a garlic taste with the cheesy parmesan addition is perfect dish for your whole family.

Preparation Time: 10 Minutes

Cooking Time: 5 Minutes

Yield: 2 Servings

Ingredients

- 1 head Broccoli
- 3 teaspoons of Olive Oil
- 4 cloves Garlic
- Salt and black pepper, to taste
- 1/3 cup Parmesan fresh grated, vegan parmesan

Directions

1.Wash the broccoli and pat dry with a paper towel.

2.Cut the broccoli into the in florets.

3.Put the broccoli in a bowl, and add garlic and olive oil.

4.Toss the broccoli well.

5.Season the broccoli with salt and black pepper and put into the Instant Omni plus air fryer toaster oven baking tray.

6.Cook for 5 minutes at 400 degrees Fahrenheit.

7.Once done, put the grated Parmesan cheese on the top.

8.Serve.

Nutrition Facts

Servings: 2

Amount per serving

Calories 220

% Daily Value*

Total Fat 19.3g 25%

Saturated Fat 7g 35%

Cholesterol 0mg 0%

Sodium 191mg 8%

Total Carbohydrate 9.4g 3%

Dietary Fiber 2.5g 9%

Total Sugars 1.6g

Protein 4.3g

Vitamin D 0mcg 0%

Calcium 107mg 8%

Iron 1mg 7%

Potassium 313mg 7%

65

AIR FRYER TOFU

This is a crispy air fryer tofu recipe that is ultra flavorful.

Preparation Time: 10 Minutes

Cooking Time: 5 Minutes

Yield: 2 Servings

Ingredients

- 14 ounces block extra firm tofu
- 2 tablespoons avocado oil
- 4 teaspoons cornstarch
- 2 teaspoons paprika
- 1/2 teaspoon onion powder
- 2 teaspoons garlic powder
- 1/4 teaspoon black pepper
- 1/4 teaspoon salt

Directions

1.First of all, take the extra firm Tofu block and press it between two paper towels.

2.Cut the Tofu into half inches cube.

3.Coat the Tofu with avocado oil and cornstarch.

4.Next add seasoning including the paprika powder o, onions powder, garlic powder salt, and black pepper.

5.Put it into the Instant Omni plus air fryer toaster oven basket.

6.Cook for 5 minutes at 390 degrees Fahrenheit

7.Once done serve and enjoy.

Nutrition Facts

Servings: 2

Amount per serving

Calories 345

% Daily Value*

Total Fat 19.4g 25%

Saturated Fat 2.9g 15%

Cholesterol 0mg 0%

Sodium 321mg 14%

Total Carbohydrate 18g 7%

Dietary Fiber 6.4g 23%

Total Sugars 1.2g

Protein 32.4g

Vitamin D 0mcg 0%

Calcium 1366mg 105%

Iron 6mg 34%

Potassium 604mg 13%

66

MALT VINEGAR CHIPS

It is the best alternative to artificially flavored chips.

Preparation Time: 10 Minutes

Cooking Time: 15 Minutes

Yield: 2 Servings

Ingredients

- 8 ounces baby spinach
- Cooking spray
- 1/4 teaspoon of malt vinegar powder

Directions

1.Wash the spinach and then pat dry with a paper towel

2.Let it sit completely to dry off.

3.Transfer it to bowl and add malt vinegar powder.

4.Oil sprays the pan of air fryer and add in the spinach.

5.Let it cook for 15 minutes at 390 degrees F , inside an Instant Omni plus air fryer toaster oven.

6.Serve.

Nutrition Facts

Servings: 2

Amount per serving

Calories 29

% Daily Value*
Total Fat 0.7g 1%
Saturated Fat 0.1g 1%
Cholesterol 0mg 0%
Sodium 90mg 4%
Total Carbohydrate 4.1g 1%
Dietary Fiber 2.5g 9%
Total Sugars 0.5g
Protein 3.2g
Vitamin D 0mcg 0%
Calcium 112mg 9%
Iron 3mg 17%
Potassium 633mg 13%

67

PARMESAN ZUCCHINI CHIPS

It is a perfect light snack to enjoy, with some great taste and health.

Preparation Time: 10 Minutes

Cooking Time: 12 Minutes

Yield: 2 Servings

Ingredients

- 2 medium zucchinis, trimmed
- 2 teaspoons kosher salt
- 2 eggs, beaten
- 2 tablespoons Water
- 1-1/2 cup Panko breadcrumbs
- 1/2 cup finely grated Parmesan cheese, vegan
- 1 teaspoon smoked paprika

Side Servings

- Ranch, for dipping

Directions

1. The first step is to wash and slice the zucchini into the round thin pieces.

2. Take a bowl and rest again it along with water.

3.Take another bowl and combine cheese, Paprika, and bread crumbs.

4.Whisk egg with salt in another bowl.

5.Dry zucchini with a paper towel and dredge it into the egg mixture then into the bread crumb mixture.

6.Once all the zucchini slices are coated, put them onto the oil grease cooking tray.

7.Place the dripping Pan at the bottom of the cooking chamber.

8.Now put the cooking tray into the Instant Omni plus air fryer toaster oven and air fry for 12 minutes at 375 degrees Fahrenheit.

9.Once done, serve.

Nutrition Facts

Servings: 2

Amount per serving

Calories 237

% Daily Value*

Total Fat 6.7g 9%

Saturated Fat 1.5g 8%

Cholesterol 164mg 55%

Sodium 2907mg 126%

Total Carbohydrate 35.4g 13%

Dietary Fiber 6.2g 22%

Total Sugars 2.9g

Protein 10.8g

Vitamin D 15mcg 77%

Calcium 38mg 3%

Iron 5mg 25%

Potassium 312mg 7%

68

BALSAMIC-PANCETTA BRUSSELS SPROUTS

This simple vegetable recipe is full of flavor and texture; it is no doubt a nutritious and healthy recipe to enjoy at lunch or dinner time.

Preparation Time: 10 Minutes

Cooking Time: 20 Minutes

Yield: 4 Servings

Ingredients

- 1 pound Brussels sprouts ends trimmed and cut into bite-sized pieces
- 2 teaspoons olive oil
- 1 tablespoon balsamic vinegar
- 3 ounce thick-sliced pancetta cut into 1/2 inch dice
- 1 cup parmesan cheese, vegan version
- Salt and black pepper, to taste

Directions

1. Take a bowls and add Brussels sprouts, olive oil, vinegar, salt, and black pepper.

2. Toss the ingredients well and then add pancetta.

3. Put this mixture into the rotisserie basket and attach the lid.

4.Place the dripping Pan at the bottom of the cooking chamber.

5.Switch the temperature at 350 degrees for height for 20 minutes

6.Lift the basket into the cooking chamber.

7.Secured the basket and close the door.

8.Cook the Brussels sprouts until golden brown, inside Instant Omni plus air fryer toaster oven.

9.Serve hot with Parmesan cheese topping

Nutrition Facts

Servings: 4

Amount per serving

Calories 357

% Daily Value*

Total Fat 29.8g 38%

Saturated Fat 12.3g 62%

Cholesterol 23mg 8%

Sodium 755mg 33%

Total Carbohydrate 10.4g 4%

Dietary Fiber 3g 11%

Total Sugars 2g

Protein 12.8g

Vitamin D 0mcg 0%

Calcium 124mg 10%

Iron 2mg 14%

Potassium 483mg 10%

69

DEHYDRATED SPICED CAULIFLOWER "POPCORN"

The dehydration is no more boring as we use Omni air fryer to dehydrate cauliflower until crispy.

Preparation Time: 10 Minutes

Cooking Time: 12 hours

Yield: 4 Servings

Ingredients

- 2 pounds head of cauliflower
- 2 tablespoons hot sauce like buffalo sauce or Frank's
- 1 tablespoon oil
- 1 teaspoon lime juice
- 1 teaspoon smoked paprika
- 1 teaspoon cumin
- 1/2 teaspoon nutmeg

Directions

1.First of all, wash the Cauliflower and pat dry with a paper towel.

2.Cut the cauliflower into florets and then put it in a large bowl.

3.Add all the remaining list ingredients, and toss the ingredients well, so that the ingredient coat evenly.

4.Put the ingredients into the cooking tray.

5.Put tray into the upper rack of the instant Omni plus air fryer toaster oven.

6.Select the dehydrate and set the timer for 12 hours, at 130 degrees Fahrenheit.

7.Once it's done serve immediately.

Nutrition Facts

Servings: 4

Amount per serving

Calories 42

% Daily Value*

Total Fat 3.8g 5%

Saturated Fat 0.6g 3%

Cholesterol 0mg 0%

Sodium 76mg 3%

Total Carbohydrate 1.9g 1%

Dietary Fiber 1g 4%

Total Sugars 0.7g

Protein 0.8g

Vitamin D 0mcg 0%

Calcium 11mg 1%

Iron 1mg 3%

Potassium 67mg 1%

70

AIR FRYER POLENTA BITES

It is a perfect vegan recipe to enjoy that is loved by whole family members.

Preparation Time: 10 Minutes

Cooking Time: 12 Minutes

Yield: 2 Servings

Ingredients

- 1 packet Polenta cut in round shapes
- 1/4 cup potato starch
- Oil spray, for greasing

Topping Ingredients

- 1/2 cup maple syrup

Directions

1.First, coat the polenta shapes with potato starch and layer it on a cooking sheet that is grease with oil spray.

2.Spray the polenta with oil as well.

3.Cook at 390 degrees F for 12 minutes in the Instant Omni plus air fryer toaster oven.

4.After 8 minutes, flip the Polenta Balls and cook for 4 minutes.

5.Serve with maple syrup as a drizzle.

Nutrition Facts
Servings: 2
Amount per serving
Calories 391
% Daily Value*
Total Fat 0.9g 1%
Saturated Fat 0.1g 0%
Cholesterol 0mg 0%
Sodium 9mg 0%
Total Carbohydrate 93g 34%
Dietary Fiber 1.3g 5%
Total Sugars 47.4g
Protein 3.8g
Vitamin D 0mcg 0%
Calcium 53mg 4%
Iron 1mg 5%
Potassium 161mg 3%

71

ZUCCHINI WITH STUFFING

These stuffed zucchinis are easy to prepare and taste great.

Preparation Time: 25 Minutes

Cooking Time: 30 Minutes

Yield: 4 Servings

Ingredients

- 1-1/2 cup quinoa, rinsed
- 1/2 cup black olives
- 1.5 cups cooked minced beef
- 4 medium zucchinis
- 1.5 cups cannellini beans, drained
- 2 white onions, chopped
- 1/2 cup almonds, chopped
- 2 cloves of garlic, chopped
- 6 tablespoons olive oil
- 1 cup of water
- 1-1/2 cups vegan cheese, mozzarella

Directions

1.First of all wash and pat dry the zucchinis.

2.Cut zucchini lengthwise.

3.Take a Skillet and heat oil in it.

4.Sauté the onions in oil along with garlic for about 2 minutes until Aroma comes.

5.Then add in water along with quinoa.

6.Cook for 10 minutes at low heat.

7.Transfer this mixture into the bowl and add all the remaining listed ingredients excluding cheese and zucchini.

8.Scoop out the seed from the zucchini.

9.Fill the Cavity of zucchini with the prepared mixture.

10. Put the Zucchini into the baking tray and added to the Instant Omni plus air fryer toaster oven cooking chamber.

11. Cook for 15 minutes at 390 degrees Fahrenheit.

12. Once done, serve and enjoy.

Nutrition Facts

Servings: 4

Amount per serving

Calories 1044

% Daily Value*

Total Fat 44.2g 57%

Saturated Fat 8.3g 41%

Cholesterol 152mg 51%

Sodium 331mg 14%

Total Carbohydrate 85.5g 31%

Dietary Fiber 26.1g 93%

Total Sugars 7.8g

Protein 80.1g

Vitamin D 0mcg 0%

Calcium 224mg 17%

Iron 41mg 230%

Potassium 2584mg 55%

72

BRUSSELS SPROUTS RECIPE

It is a simple and clean vegan recipe.

Preparation Time: 25 Minutes

Cooking Time: 25 Minutes

Yield: 3 Servings

Ingredients

- 1.5 pounds Brussels sprouts
- 2 tablespoons vegetable oil
- Salt and pepper, to taste
- 1 teaspoon of turmeric

Directions

1.Wash the Brussels sprouts and trim the bottom of it.

2.Take a bowl and mix Brussels sprouts, oil, salt, pepper, and turmeric.

3.Transfer the Brussels sprout into an air fryer basket.

4.Put the dripping Pan beneath the Instant Omni plus air fryer toaster oven basket.

5.Cook it for 25 minutes at 390 degrees Fahrenheit.

6.Serve and enjoy.

Nutrition Facts

Servings: 3

Amount per serving

Calories 181

% Daily Value*

Total Fat 9.9g 13%

Saturated Fat 2.1g 10%

Cholesterol 0mg 0%

Sodium 57mg 2%

Total Carbohydrate 21.1g 8%

Dietary Fiber 8.7g 31%

Total Sugars 4.9g

Protein 7.8g

Vitamin D 0mcg 0%

Calcium 79mg 6%

Iron 3mg 17%

Potassium 900mg 19%

73

EGGPLANTS SATAY

A classic vegan recipe to try with some healthy ingredients combination.

Preparation Time: 15 Minutes
Cooking Time: 16 Minutes
Yield: 2 Servings
Ingredients
- 2 large eggplants, center cored
- 1/3 cup cornstarch+1/4 cups water
- 2 tablespoons of Olive Oil
- Pinch of sea salt
- 1/2 cup tomatoes
- 1/2 cup chopped mint leaves
- 1/2 teaspoon of ginger garlic paste
- 1 large onion, chopped

Directions
1.The first step is to wash the eggplants.

2.Cut the top of the eggplant and center core the eggplant.

3.The next step is to heat oil in a skillet and sauté onions along with ginger and garlic paste.

4.Add tomato and mint leaf along with salt in the skillet.

5.Mix cornstarch with water and added it to the Skillet as well.

6.Let it cook for 5 minutes.

7.Now fill the cavity of the eggplant with the prepared mixture from the Skillet.

8.Transfer the eggplant into the air fryer baking tray and cook for 16 minutes at 390 degrees Fahrenheit, inside Instant Omni plus air fryer toaster oven.

9.Once done serve and enjoy.

Nutrition Facts

Servings: 2

Amount per serving

Calories 305

% Daily Value*

Total Fat 15.3g 20%

Saturated Fat 2.1g 10%

Cholesterol 0mg 0%

Sodium 140mg 6%

Total Carbohydrate 42.9g 16%

Dietary Fiber 23g 82%

Total Sugars 20.8g

Protein 7.4g

Vitamin D 0mcg 0%

Calcium 116mg 9%

Iron 4mg 24%

Potassium 1576mg 34%

74

SPINACH QUICHE

A very healthy recipe to enjoy at breakfast

Preparation Time: 15 Minutes

Cooking Time: 10minutes

Yield: 6 Servings

Ingredients

- 6 eggs
- 1 cup spinach
- 1 cup heavy cream
- 2 tablespoons honey mustard
- 1/2 cup grated Swiss cheese
- 1 teaspoon thyme
- Pinch salt and freshly ground black pepper

Directions

1. Take a large bowl and cracked egg.

2. Whisk the egg along with all the meaning listed ingredients.

3. Transfer the egg mixture into the greased baking pan air fry chamber and cook for 10 minutes at 390 degrees Fahrenheit, inside Instant Omni plus air fryer toaster oven.

4. Once done, serve and enjoy.

Nutrition Facts

Servings: 6
Amount per serving
Calories 178
% Daily Value*
Total Fat 14.3g 18%
Saturated Fat 7.6g 38%
Cholesterol 199mg 66%
Sodium 116mg 5%
Total Carbohydrate 3.7g 1%
Dietary Fiber 0.2g 1%
Total Sugars 1.5g
Protein 8.5g
Vitamin D 30mcg 149%
Calcium 116mg 9%
Iron 1mg 7%
Potassium 110mg 2%

75

SQUASH WITH CUMIN AND CHILI

A recipe rich in vitamins, minerals and protein.

Preparation Time: 25 Minutes

Cooking Time: 20 Minutes

Yield: 3 Servings

Ingredients

- 3 butternut squash
- 5 tablespoons of cumin seeds
- 1 teaspoon of chili flakes
- 1 tablespoon of olive oil
- 1-1/2 cups plain Greek yogurt
- 1/2 cup pine nuts

Directions

1.Wash the squash and pat dry with a paper towel.

2.Sliced the squash and remove the seeds and cut into chunks.

3.Put it in the bowl and add all remaining listed ingredients, excluding Greek yogurt.

4.Now transfer the squash pieces into the Instant Omni plus air fryer toaster oven grease baking tray and cook for 20 minutes at 350 degrees Fahrenheit.

5.Remember to check the squash two or three times during the cooking processes.

6.Serve the cooked squash with a dollop of yogurt.

Nutrition Facts

Servings: 3

Amount per serving

Calories 493

% Daily Value*

Total Fat 22.5g 29%

Saturated Fat 2g 10%

Cholesterol 0mg 0%

Sodium 153mg 7%

Total Carbohydrate 37.8g 14%

Dietary Fiber 4.7g 17%

Total Sugars 18.1g

Protein 42.3g

Vitamin D 0mcg 0%

Calcium 564mg 43%

Iron 9mg 51%

Potassium 1288mg 27%

APPETIZERS RECIPES

76

EGGPLANT FRIES

It is a very easy recipe to prepare with some whole ingredients added to recipes.

Preparation Time: 15 Minutes
Cooking Time: 15 Minutes
Yield: 4 Servings
Ingredients

- 4 large eggplants, thinly sliced
- Salt, to taste
- 2 teaspoons of red chilies
- 1/2 teaspoon of coriander
- 1/ teaspoon of baking powder
- 1 teaspoon of dry pomegranate seeds
- 1 cup chickpea flour
- 1 cup of water

Directions

1.Pour water in a bowl and add chickpea flour, baking powder, salt, coriander, red chili, and dry pomegranate seed as well.

2.Mix ingredients to make a smooth paste.

3.Then dredge all the eggplants into and mix to coat well.

4.Put the eggplant into the Instant Omni plus air fryer toaster oven basket and let it cook at 390 degrees until brown on top for about 15 minutes.

    5.Serve it immediately.

Nutrition Facts

Servings: 4

Amount per serving

Calories 320

% Daily Value*

Total Fat 4g 5%

Saturated Fat 0.3g 2%

Cholesterol 0mg 0%

Sodium 64mg 3%

Total Carbohydrate 62.8g 23%

Dietary Fiber 28.2g 101%

Total Sugars 22g

Protein 15.1g

Vitamin D 0mcg 0%

Calcium 104mg 8%

Iron 4mg 24%

Potassium 1701mg 36%

77

BACON TATER TOTS

It is a recipe equally loved by kids and adults.

Preparation Time: 20 Minutes

Cooking Time: 14 Minutes

Yield: 5 Servings

Ingredients

- 20 frozen tater tots
- 6 slices precooked bacon
- 6 tablespoons maple syrup
- 1/2 cup Cheddar cheese, shredded

Directions

1.Put the tater tots in air fryer baking tray and place in the cooking chamber.

2.Cook at 350 degrees F, for 8 minutes.

3.Meanwhile, chop the bacon into bite-size pieces.

4.Take out the tater tots from the air fryer.

5.Put it into a medium baking pan and add maple syrup and bacon bits.

6.Cook it in the Instant Omni plus air fryer toaster oven for 5 minutes.

7.Top it with cheese, once the cooking process is done.

8.Cook for 1 minute and then serve.

Nutrition Facts

Servings: 5

Amount per serving

Calories 454

% Daily Value*

Total Fat 24.5g 31%

Saturated Fat 2.7g 13%

Cholesterol 12mg 4%

Sodium 604mg 26%

Total Carbohydrate 51.4g 19%

Dietary Fiber 0.2g 1%

Total Sugars 14.3g

Protein 6.6g

Vitamin D 1mcg 7%

Calcium 99mg 8%

Iron 1mg 3%

Potassium 70mg 1%

78

FIGS WITH MASCARPONE

It is a recipe that provides all essential nutrients needed for body.

Preparation Time: 10 Minutes

Cooking Time: 5 Minutes

Yield: 2 Servings

Ingredients

- 8 figs
- 1/3 cup butter
- 2 tablespoons honey
- 150ml mascarpone
- 1 teaspoon of almonds, to serve
- A Few teaspoons of Rosewater, as per needed

Directions

1. Make a slit on the top of each fig and open it with a squeeze.

2. Put the figs in a baking dish and put butter on each of figs.

3. Drizzle a generous amount of honey as well.

4. Cook it in the Instant Omni plus air fryer toaster oven, basket and cook for 5 minutes.

5. Meanwhile, in a bowl combine rosewater into the mascarpone.

6.Once figs are done put a dollop of mascarpone on each caramelized fig.

7.Garnish it off with almonds.

8.Serve and enjoy.

Nutrition Facts

Servings: 2

Amount per serving

Calories 667

% Daily Value*

Total Fat 42.1g 54%

Saturated Fat 26.1g 131%

Cholesterol 121mg 40%

Sodium 292mg 13%

Total Carbohydrate 68.5g 25%

Dietary Fiber 7.6g 27%

Total Sugars 53.9g

Protein 12g

Vitamin D 21mcg 106%

Calcium 299mg 23%

Iron 2mg 11%

Potassium 627mg 13%

79

CHEESE BALLS

A very aromatic recipe to enjoy any time you like.

Preparation Time: 10 Minutes

Cooking Time: `15 Minutes

Yield: 3 Servings

Ingredients

- 1/2 cup of rice
- 1/2 cup Indian cottage cheese, grated
- 1 cups carrots
- 1/2 cup sweet corn
- 1/2 cup mozzarella cheese
- 1/2 cup corn flour
- 1/3 cup breadcrumbs
- 1/2 teaspoon of garlic powder
- 1/2 teaspoon of Italian seasoning

Directions

1.Mix all the listed ingredients in a bowl, excluding breadcrumbs.

2.Roll mixture into small balls.

3.Roll the ball into bread crumbs and place it into an air fryer basket.

4.Cook for 15 minutes at 390 degrees F, inside Instant Omni plus air fryer toaster oven.

5.Serve.

Nutrition Facts

Servings: 3

Amount per serving

Calories 319

% Daily Value*

Total Fat 3.7g 5%

Saturated Fat 1.4g 7%

Cholesterol 6mg 2%

Sodium 301mg 13%

Total Carbohydrate 58.7g 21%

Dietary Fiber 4g 14%

Total Sugars 3.8g

Protein 12.9g

Vitamin D 0mcg 0%

Calcium 74mg 6%

Iron 3mg 18%

Potassium 349mg 7%

80

PRAWNS SNACK

A recipe that is prepared with readily available ingredients.

Preparation Time: 6 Minutes

Cooking Time: 8 Minutes

Yield: 2 Servings

Ingredients

- 8 fresh king prawns
- 1/3 tablespoon of wine vinegar
- 2 tablespoons of mayonnaise
- 2 teaspoons of ketchup
- 1 teaspoon chili flakes
- Salt and black pepper, to taste

Directions

1.In a bowl, mix wine vinegar, mayonnaise, ketchup, chili flakes, salt, and black pepper.

2.Add the prawns to the mix and coat them well.

3.Place the prawns into the frying basket, and cook for 8 minutes at 350 degrees F, inside Instant Omni plus air fryer toaster oven.

4.Serve as an appetizer.

Nutrition Facts

Servings: 2
Amount per serving
Calories 167
% Daily Value*
Total Fat 6.4g 8%
Saturated Fat 1.2g 6%
Cholesterol 189mg 63%
Sodium 375mg 16%
Total Carbohydrate 6.2g 2%
Dietary Fiber 0g 0%
Total Sugars 2.1g
Protein 20.3g
Vitamin D 0mcg 0%
Calcium 83mg 6%
Iron 0mg 2%
Potassium 172mg 4%

81

YELLOW SQUASH FRITTERS

It is a delicious recipe to enjoy.

Preparation Time: 10 Minutes

Cooking Time: 12 Minutes

Yield: 4 Servings

Ingredients

- 4 ounces Cream cheese
- 1 egg, beaten
- 1 teaspoon oregano, dried
- 3 small yellow summer squash, grated
- 1 cup carrots, grated
- 4 tablespoons olive oil
- Salt and black pepper, to taste

Directions

1.In a medium bowl and combine all the listed ingredients, excluding oil.

2.Form the patties with wet hands.

3.Brush the fritters with olive oil.

4.Put in oil greased baking tray and put in the air fryer chamber.

5.Cook in the air fryer for 12 minutes at 350 degrees F, inside Instant Omni plus air fryer toaster oven.

6.Serve and enjoy.

Nutrition Facts

Servings: 4

Amount per serving

Calories 261

% Daily Value*

Total Fat 25g 32%

Saturated Fat 8.6g 43%

Cholesterol 72mg 24%

Sodium 333mg 14%

Total Carbohydrate 7.3g 3%

Dietary Fiber 2.2g 8%

Total Sugars 3g

Protein 4.4g

Vitamin D 4mcg 19%

Calcium 45mg 3%

Iron 3mg 16%

Potassium 371mg 8%

82

PRAWN SPRING ROLLS

It is a perfect lunch or dinner time recipe to prepare.

Preparation Time: 10 Minutes

Cooking Time: 6 Minutes

Yield: 4 Servings

Ingredients

- 2 tablespoons of vegetable oil
- 2 tablespoons of soy sauce
- 1 teaspoon of root ginger
- 50 grams of mushrooms, sliced
- 30 grams of water chestnuts, sliced
- 1/2 teaspoon of five-spice powder
- 40 grams bean sprouts
- 2 spring onions
- 2 carrots cut into matchsticks
- 120 grams cooked prawns
- 10 spring roll wrappers
- 2 eggs, beaten
- Oil Spray, For Greasing

Directions

1.Heat vegetable oil in a skillet over medium flame, then add ginger, water, chestnuts, and mushrooms, and cook it for 4 minutes.

2.Next add the soy sauce, five-spice powder, spring onions, sprouts, prawns, and carrot.

3.Cook for 5 more minutes.

4.Roll up this prepared mixture into wrappers, once cool seal the sides with beaten egg.

5.Brush the rice rolls with oil.

6.Layer in air frying baking tray that is greased with oil spray.

7.Cook for about 12 minutes at 400 degrees F, inside Instant Omni plus air fryer toaster oven.

8.Flip halfway through.

9.Serve and enjoy afterward.

Nutrition Facts

Servings: 4

Amount per serving

Calories 398

% Daily Value*

Total Fat 11g 14%

Saturated Fat 2.4g 12%

Cholesterol 152mg 51%

Sodium 1037mg 45%

Total Carbohydrate 54.6g 20%

Dietary Fiber 2.6g 9%

Total Sugars 2.2g

Protein 19.3g

Vitamin D 53mcg 264%

Calcium 97mg 7%

Iron 4mg 23%

Potassium 365mg 8%

83

AIR FRYER POPCORN CHICKEN

It is a family-approved recipe to enjoy.

Preparation Time: 14 Minutes

Cooking Time: 12 Minutes

Yield: 2 servings

Ingredients

- 1 pound chicken breasts, cubed, bite-sized pieces
- 1/3 cup cornstarch
- 1 egg, for egg wash
- 1 teaspoon garlic powder
- 1/2 teaspoon onion powder
- 1 teaspoon paprika
- 1/2 cup all purpose flour
- Cooking spray, for greasing
- Salt, to taste
- 1/3 cup buttermilk

Directions

1. Mix all the spices with corn flour and all purpose flour in a bowl.

2. Cut the breasts in bite-size pieces.

3. Add it to buttermilk.

4.Then dredge into the flour mixture.

5.Whisk the egg in a medium bowl and dip the chicken to coat in egg wash.

6.Add the chicken into the flour mixture again and coat well.

7.Shake off excess flour.

8.Spray the chicken with oil spray.

9.Add the chicken to the rotisserie basket and close.

10. Set the air fryer at 370 degrees for 12 minutes, inside Instant Omni plus air fryer toaster oven.

11. Afterward, remove and serve.

Nutrition Facts

Servings: 2

Amount per serving

Calories 686

% Daily Value*

Total Fat 20.1g 26%

Saturated Fat 5.6g 28%

Cholesterol 285mg 95%

Sodium 350mg 15%

Total Carbohydrate 47.5g 17%

Dietary Fiber 1.6g 6%

Total Sugars 2.9g

Protein 73.5g

Vitamin D 8mcg 39%

Calcium 103mg 8%

Iron 5mg 28%

Potassium 722mg 15%

84

STUFFED TOMATOES

A recipe that is perfect in texture and delicious in taste.

Preparation Time: 20 Minutes

Cooking Time: 20 Minutes

Yield: 2 Servings

Ingredients

- 2.5 cups wild rice, cooked
- 2 pounds grilled chicken breasts cut into pieces
- 2 large red tomatoes
- 2 tablespoons fresh basil
- 2 tablespoons olive oil
- Black pepper, to taste
- Pinch of sea salt
- 2 tablespoons of lemon juice
- 2 teaspoons of red chili powder
- 3 jalapeños, chopped

Directions

1.In a large bowl and combine rice, salt, pepper, basil, chicken meat, oil, chilies, lemon, and jalapeño in it.

2.Next, center core the tomatoes.

3.Fill the cavity with a prepared mixture.

4.Oil greases the air fryer pan and put in the tomatoes.

5.Bake in the air fryer for 20 minutes at 390 degrees F, inside Instant Omni plus air fryer toaster oven.

6.Serve and enjoy.

Nutrition Facts

Servings: 2

Amount per serving

Calories 1364

% Daily Value*

Total Fat 28.1g 36%

Saturated Fat 2.5g 13%

Cholesterol 290mg 97%

Sodium 392mg 17%

Total Carbohydrate 151.6g 55%

Dietary Fiber 13.4g 48%

Total Sugars 5.5g

Protein 126.2g

Vitamin D 0mcg 1%

Calcium 78mg 6%

Iron 6mg 34%

Potassium 2609mg 56%

85

AIR FRIED POTATOES

Is a recipe that combines health in one dish?

Preparation Time: 10 Minutes

Cooking Time: 40 Minutes

Yield: 2 Servings

Ingredients

- 3 russet potatoes, un-peeled
- 1/2 tablespoons melted butter
- Salt, to taste
- 1/2 teaspoon garlic powder
- 1 cup sour cream

Directions

1.First wash and pat dry the potatoes.

2.Then prick potatoes with a fork.

3.Coat the potatoes with butter.

4.Sprinkle with sea salt and garlic powder evenly.

5.Put the drip pan at the bottom of the cooking chamber of Instant Omni plus air fryer toaster oven.

6.Adjust the temperature to 400 degrees F, and set the timer to 40 minutes.

7.Add potatoes on a tray and close door.

8.Afterward, remove baked potatoes and serve with sour cream.

Nutrition Facts

Servings: 2

Amount per serving

Calories 421

% Daily Value*

Total Fat 27.2g 35%

Saturated Fat 16.9g 84%

Cholesterol 58mg 19%

Sodium 172mg 7%

Total Carbohydrate 38.9g 14%

Dietary Fiber 5.2g 19%

Total Sugars 2.8g

Protein 7.4g

Vitamin D 2mcg 10%

Calcium 154mg 12%

Iron 1mg 7%

Potassium 1041mg 22%

SNACKS AND DESSERTS

86

OMNI AIR FRYER OREOS

These are super easy Oreo dessert time recipe that is prepared with a crescent roll.

Preparation Time: 10 Minutes

Cooking Time: 6 Minutes

Yield: 4 Servings

Ingredients

- 4 packs crescent roll dough, premade
- 4-5 Oreo cookies
- 2 tablespoons of powdered sugar, sprinkling
- Oil spray, for greasing

Directions

1. Taken air fryer basket and grease it with oil spray.

2. Take the Oreo cookie and wrap each of it with the Crescent roll dough.

3. Trim any access dough.

4. Place it in the Instant Omni plus air fryer toaster oven, and cook for 6 minutes at 390 degrees Fahrenheit.

5. After 3 minutes of cooking, flip cookies to cook from the other side.

6.Once it's golden brown from the top sprinkle powdered sugar on top and serve.

Nutrition Facts

Servings: 4

Amount per serving

Calories 163

% Daily Value*

Total Fat 8.1g 10%

Saturated Fat 2.9g 14%

Cholesterol 0mg 0%

Sodium 268mg 12%

Total Carbohydrate 22.1g 8%

Dietary Fiber 0.3g 1%

Total Sugars 10g

Protein 1.5g

Vitamin D 0mcg 0%

Calcium 2mg 0%

Iron 1mg 6%

Potassium 149mg 3%

87

AIR FRYER APPLE CHIPS

These are the best alternative to any packed snack items and satisfy your sweet tooth with its crispy and delicious taste.

Preparation Time: 15 Minutes

Cooking Time: 10 Minutes

Yield: 2 Servings

Ingredients

- 2 large sweet, crisp apples, Honey crisp
- 1/2 teaspoon ground cinnamon
- 1/4 teaspoon of salt

Directions

1. Wash and pat dry the apples.

2. Centre core the apples to remove the seeds.

3. Use a short knife and cut the apple sideways into thin round slices.

4. Combine Cinnamon and salt in a bowl.

5. Sprinkle the Cinnamon and salt over the apple slices.

6. Take an air fryer baking tray and arrange the apples in a single layer in it.

7. Air fry in Instant Omni plus air fryer toaster oven, at 390 degrees Fahrenheit for about 10 minutes.

8.Remember to flip the Apple Halfway through.

9.Once the desired crispiness is achieved, takeout and cool it over a cooling rack.

10. Serve and enjoy.

Nutrition Facts

Servings: 2

Amount per serving

Calories 117

% Daily Value*

Total Fat 0.4g 1%

Saturated Fat 0g 0%

Cholesterol 0mg 0%

Sodium 293mg 13%

Total Carbohydrate 31.3g 11%

Dietary Fiber 5.7g 20%

Total Sugars 23.2g

Protein 0.6g

Vitamin D 0mcg 0%

Calcium 7mg 1%

Iron 1mg 6%

Potassium 241mg 5%

88

AIR FRYER KALE CHIPS

The best cooking technique for crispy, bright green kale chips is provided in this recipe.

Preparation Time: 15 Minutes

Cooking Time: 7 Minutes

Yield: 2 Servings

Ingredients

- 6 ounces of kale, torn into 2" pieces
- 1 tablespoon olive oil
- 2 teaspoons everything bagel seasoning

Directions

1.Place the torn kale in a large bowl and drizzle olive oil on top.

2.Then Sprinkle the Bagel seasoning.

3.Toss the ingredients for a fine combination.

4.Place the ingredients on to the cooking tray.

5.Air fry the Kale for 7 minutes at 350 degrees Fahrenheit in the Instant Omni plus air fryer toaster oven.

6.Keep an eye on the kale, as you need to remove the chips that start turning brown.

7.Once the cooking process is complete remove the chips and serve.

Nutrition Facts

Servings: 2

Amount per serving

Calories 102

% Daily Value*

Total Fat 7g 9%

Saturated Fat 1g 5%

Cholesterol 0mg 0%

Sodium 37mg 2%

Total Carbohydrate 8.9g 3%

Dietary Fiber 1.3g 5%

Total Sugars 0g

Protein 2.5g

Vitamin D 0mcg 0%

Calcium 114mg 9%

Iron 1mg 8%

Potassium 418mg 9%

89

AIR FRYER SWEET POTATO CHIPS

It is a very healthy and nutritious snack to enjoy, which is perfectly addictive.

Preparation Time: 15 Minutes

Cooking Time: 15-30 Minutes

Yield: 2 Servings

Ingredients

- 1-2 medium sweet potato, cut into 1/8-inch-thick slices
- 2 tablespoons canola oil
- 1/3teaspoon sea salt
- 1/3 teaspoon freshly ground black pepper
- 1 teaspoon chopped fresh rosemary
- Oil spray, for greasing

Directions

1.Keep the sweet potatoes unpeeled.

2.Take a bowl and pour cold water into it.

3.Soak sweet potato slices in the cold water for 20 minutes.

4.After 20 minutes pat dry the potato slices.

5.Sprinkle salt, pepper, and Rosemary on the potato slices.

6.At the end drizzle a generous amount of oil.

7.Take a basket and grease it with cooking spray.

8.Place the coated sweet potatoes in the Instant Omni plus air fryer toaster oven basket.

9.Cook in batches at 350 degrees Fahrenheit, for about 15 minutes for one batch.

10. Afterward, remove the sweet potatoes from the air fly.

11. Let it sit to get cool.

12. Then serve and enjoy.

Nutrition Facts

Servings: 2

Amount per serving

Calories 181

% Daily Value*

Total Fat 14.5g 19%

Saturated Fat 1.1g 6%

Cholesterol 0mg 0%

Sodium 21mg 1%

Total Carbohydrate 12.4g 5%

Dietary Fiber 2.3g 8%

Total Sugars 3.7g

Protein 1.2g

Vitamin D 0mcg 0%

Calcium 11mg 1%

Iron 2mg 13%

Potassium 281mg 6%

90

AIR FRYER PIZZA

It is a perfect snack time pizza that is light and nutritious at the same time. Try this recipe to make the delicious personal-sized pizza using Omni air fryer.

Preparation Time: 15 Minutes

Cooking Time: 12 Minutes

Yield: 2 Servings

Ingredients

- 6 ounces of Pizza dough - 5 oz
- 4 ounces Mozzarella cheese, shredded
- 1/3 cup tomato sauce
- Oil, for brushing
- Basil leaves, few

Directions

1. The first step is to prepare the pizza dough.

2. For that take the pizza dough and set it in the refrigerator for 30 minutes.

3. Afterward, take it out and let it rest.

4. Now roll the dough according to the size of the air fryer basket.

5. Brush a generous amount of oil on top.

6.Afterward, brush the tomato sauce over the dough.

7.At the end topic with cheese slices and basil leaves.

8.Air fry at 375 degrees Fahrenheit for 12 minutes, inside Instant Omni plus air fryer toaster oven.

9.Once the cheese melt and crust get golden brown, serve, and enjoy.

Nutrition Facts

Servings: 2

Amount per serving

Calories 629

% Daily Value*

Total Fat 43.1g 55%

Saturated Fat 13.4g 67%

Cholesterol 30mg 10%

Sodium 964mg 42%

Total Carbohydrate 40.2g 15%

Dietary Fiber 3.5g 13%

Total Sugars 1.9g

Protein 21.4g

Vitamin D 0mcg 0%

Calcium 53mg 4%

Iron 3mg 15%

Potassium 186mg 4%

91

CINNAMON BANANAS

A very nutty-tasting treat that is prepared in just 4 minutes.

Preparation Time: 5 Minutes

Cooking Time: 4 Minutes

Yield: 2 Servings

Ingredients

- Oil spray, for greasing
- 1 banana, peeled
- 2 tablespoons brown sugar
- 1 teaspoon ground cinnamon

Directions

1. Use ripe bananas and peel them.

2. Cut in round cubes.

3. Grease an air fryer tray with oil spray.

4. Sprinkle sugar and cinnamon on top.

5. Air fry for 4 minutes at 400 degrees F, inside Instant Omni plus air fryer toaster oven.

6. Once done, take out and serve as a snack.

Nutrition Facts

Servings: 2

Amount per serving

Calories 92
% Daily Value*
Total Fat 0.5g 1%
Saturated Fat 0.1g 1%
Cholesterol 0mg 0%
Sodium 3mg 0%
Total Carbohydrate 23.2g 8%
Dietary Fiber 2.1g 8%
Total Sugars 16g
Protein 0.7g
Vitamin D 0mcg 0%
Calcium 22mg 2%
Iron 0mg 2%
Potassium 228mg 5%

92

AIR FRYER BUFFALO CAULIFLOWER

It is a very easy and low calories snack to enjoy in the evening.

Preparation Time: 15 Minutes

Cooking Time: 10 Minutes

Yield: 2 Servings

Ingredients

- 2 cups of Frozen Cauliflower florets
- 4 tablespoons Cholula Hot Sauce
- Sea salt and pepper to season

Directions

1. Turn on the air fryer and select 400 degrees F.
2. Set timer to 10 minutes.
3. Put the cauliflower onto a baking tray, and place in the Instant Omni plus air fryer toaster oven.
4. Cook for 5 minutes. then take out.
5. Take a bowl and mix florets, hot sauce, salt, and black pepper.
6. Then again put it in the tray and cook for 5 more minutes.
7. Once it's done, serve.

Nutrition Facts

Servings: 2

Amount per serving

Calories 20

% Daily Value*

Total Fat 0g 0%

Saturated Fat 0g 0%

Cholesterol 0mg 0%

Sodium 20mg 1%

Total Carbohydrate 4g 1%

Dietary Fiber 2g 7%

Total Sugars 1g

Protein 1g

Vitamin D 0mcg 0%

Calcium 20mg 2%

Iron 0mg 0%

Potassium 0mg 0%

93

BAKED APPLES

It is very easy and fun to make recipe equally loved by kids and adults. It can serve as a healthy dessert for the whole family.

Preparation Time: 15 Minutes

Cooking Time: 20 Minutes

Yield: 2 Servings

Ingredients

- 2 apples
- 4 tablespoons walnuts
- 4 tablespoons raisins
- 2 tablespoons butter
- 4 tablespoons oats, quick oats
- 1/4 teaspoon of ground cinnamon
- 1/4 teaspoon of ground nutmeg

Directions

1.Center core the apples and cut the top off.

2.Make the filling by mixing raisins, walnuts, nutmeg, butter, oats, and cinnamon.

3.Scoop the filling into the center of the apple.

4.Cook for 20 minutes at 370 degrees F, inside Instant Omni plus air fryer toaster oven.

5.Plate, serve, and enjoy!

Nutrition Facts

Servings: 2

Amount per serving

Calories 409

% Daily Value*

Total Fat 22g 28%

Saturated Fat 8g 40%

Cholesterol 31mg 10%

Sodium 87mg 4%

Total Carbohydrate 54g 20%

Dietary Fiber 8.4g 30%

Total Sugars 34.3g

Protein 6.4g

Vitamin D 8mcg 40%

Calcium 32mg 2%

Iron 2mg 13%

Potassium 499mg 11%

94

PINEAPPLE IN AIR FRYER

It is a very simple and easy treat that is the best alternative to any cracker out there.

Preparation Time: 5 Minutes

Cooking Time: 12 Minutes

Yield: 3 Servings

Ingredients

- 1 large pineapple, cut into round slices
- Salt, to taste

Directions

- Sprinkle the pineapple slices with salt.
- Place in an Instant Omni plus air fryer toaster oven basket and cook for 12 minutes at 390 degrees F.
- Once done, serve as a yummy snack.

Nutrition Facts

Servings: 3

Amount per serving

Calories 82

% Daily Value*

Total Fat 0.2g 0%

Saturated Fat 0g 0%

Cholesterol 0mg 0%
Sodium 52mg 2%
Total Carbohydrate 21.7g 8%
Dietary Fiber 2.3g 8%
Total Sugars 16.3g
Protein 0.9g
Vitamin D 0mcg 0%
Calcium 21mg 2%
Iron 0mg 3%
Potassium 180mg 4%

95

AIR FRYER CHOCOLATE CHIP COOKIES

If you are a chocolate lover and lukewarm cookies as a dessert, then this recipe is for you.

Preparation Time: 15 Minutes

Cooking Time: 6 Minutes

Yield: 4 Servings

Ingredients

- 1 cup unsalted butter
- 3/4 cup granulated sugar
- 3/4 cup brown sugar
- 2 tablespoons vanilla extract
- 2 large eggs
- Pinch of salt
- 1-1/2 teaspoon baking soda
- 2 1/2 cups all-purpose flour
- 2 cups chocolate chunks or chips
- 3/4 cup chopped walnuts

Directions

1. Use a stand mixer to blend butter to turn it soft.

2. Then add the sugar, dark brown sugar, and beat until it is fluffy.

3.Next, add the vanilla extract, eggs, salt, and beat until finely combined.

4.Now add the baking soda and all-purpose flour.

5.Make smooth dough and then fold in the chocolate chips.

6.At the end, stir in the walnuts.

7.Stir with a rubber spatula until finely combined.

8.Set the air fryer at 350 degrees for 5 minutes.

9.Line the air fryer racks with parchment paper.

10. Flatten scoop of dough on the rack, with space between.

11. Bake until golden brown, about 6 minutes, inside Instant Omni plus air fryer toaster oven.

12. Remove the cookies from the rack and then cool for 5 minutes.

13. Serve and enjoy.

Nutrition Facts

Servings: 4

Amount per serving

Calories 1160

% Daily Value*

Total Fat 63.9g 82%

Saturated Fat 31.1g 155%

Cholesterol 215mg 72%

Sodium 761mg 33%

Total Carbohydrate 131.7g 48%

Dietary Fiber 4g 14%

Total Sugars 67.1g

Protein 17.6g

Vitamin D 41mcg 203%

Calcium 90mg 7%

Iron 6mg 32%

Potassium 336mg 7%

BREAD, PIZZAS AND CAKES

96

BROWNIE CAKE

The use of instant pot Omni air fryer toaster makes it more delicious and healthy.

Preparation Time: 15 Minutes

Cooking Time: 20 Minutes

Yield: 2 Servings

Ingredients

- 1 Boxed Brownie Mix
- Egg, as needed
- Vegetable Oil, as needed

Directions

1. Take a mixing bowl and mix brownie mixture according to the package instruction.

2. Transfer the mixture into the squared baking Pan that is grease with oil separator.

3. Put it into the Instant Omni plus air fryer toaster oven chamber and cook it for 20 minutes at 350 degrees Fahrenheit.

4. Check the cake with a toothpick to see that if it is done or not.

5. Once the time complete take it out, cut and serve.

Nutrition Facts

Servings: 2
Amount per serving
Calories 337
% Daily Value*
Total Fat 31.4g 40%
Saturated Fat 6.5g 33%
Cholesterol 82mg 27%
Sodium 78mg 3%
Total Carbohydrate 0.2g 0%
Dietary Fiber 0.5g 2%
Total Sugars 8.2g
Protein 3.8g
Vitamin D 8mcg 39%
Calcium 12mg 1%
Iron 1mg 5%
Potassium 29mg 1%

97

AIR FRYER POUND CAKE RECIPE

It is cooked in lesser time and gives mouthwatering taste and flavors.

Preparation Time: 20minutes

Cooking Time: 45 Minutes

Yield: 4 Servings

Ingredients

- 3/4 cups all-purpose flour
- 1/3 teaspoon baking powder
- 1/ teaspoon salt
- 1/3 cup 1 stick butter, softened
- 1 cup of sugar
- 2 teaspoons lemon juice
- 2 eggs
- 2 teaspoons pure vanilla extract

Directions

1. Take a cake pan to grease it with olive oil.

2. Take a bowl and combined baking powder, salt, and flour.

3. In a separable bowl beat together butter and 1 cup of sugar with the help of a hand mixer.

4.Keep the mixture running and add one egg at a time along with vanilla.

5.Once all the eggs are been added, pour in the lemon juice and mix until the smooth.

6.Now combine the ingredients of both the bowl.

7.Pour it into the cake Pan and cook inside the Instant Omni plus air fryer toaster oven, for 45 minutes at 330 degrees Fahrenheit.

8.Once done, lets it to get cool.

9.Cut into the slices and serve.

Nutrition Facts

Servings: 4

Amount per serving

Calories 447

% Daily Value*

Total Fat 17.8g 23%

Saturated Fat 10.5g 52%

Cholesterol 123mg 41%

Sodium 141mg 6%

Total Carbohydrate 68.6g 25%

Dietary Fiber 0.7g 2%

Total Sugars 50.6g

Protein 5.4g

Vitamin D 18mcg 92%

Calcium 38mg 3%

Iron 2mg 8%

Potassium 108mg 2%

98

AIR FRYER LILLIAN'S BANANA CAKE

It is a family hit recipe that gives your taste buds a roller coaster ride of flavors.

Preparation Time: 20 Minutes

Cooking Time: 15 Minutes

Yield: 4 Servings

Ingredients

- 4 bananas very ripe
- 1/3 cup butter room temperature
- 1/2 cup of sugar
- 3 eggs
- 1 cup cream
- 5 tablespoons Buttermilk
- 1 teaspoon baking soda
- 1/8 Teaspoon salt
- 2 cups all-purpose flour
- 1-1/2 cups walnuts chopped

Directions

1.Take a bowl and put a mesh strainer on it.

2.Place a few pieces of banana in the strainer.

3.Push the bananas through the strainer so it gets mashed.

4.Once bananas are being mashed, add half a cup of butter, half a cup sugar, and cream.

5.Now user hand beater to combine all the ingredients to form a creamy texture.

6.Add beaten eggs into the bowl and incorporate well.

7.Next, add buttermilk and baking soda along with all-purpose flour.

8.Add a Pinch of salt and use a spatula to mix down all the ingredients.

9.Add chopped walnuts and fold into the mixture.

10. Grease a cake pan with oil spray and pour the cake mixture into the pan.

11. Place it in an Instant Omni plus air fryer toaster oven chamber and bake it at 320 degrees Fahrenheit for 15 minutes.

12. Press the start and allow the cooking process to complete.

13. Allow the cake to get cool completely and then cut and serve.

Nutrition Facts
Servings: 4
Amount per serving
Calories 425
% Daily Value*
Total Fat 13.8g 18%
Saturated Fat 6.9g 35%
Cholesterol 150mg 50%
Sodium 442mg 19%
Total Carbohydrate 65.8g 24%
Dietary Fiber 1.8g 6%
Total Sugars 27.6g
Protein 11.7g
Vitamin D 16mcg 78%
Calcium 66mg 5%
Iron 3mg 17%
Potassium 154mg 3%

99

AIR FRYER CHEESY BREAD RECIPE

The combinations of ingredients are simple, yet delicious.

Preparation Time: 15 Minutes

Cooking Time: 10 Minutes

Yield: 3 Servings

Ingredients

- 5 ounces Tapioca flour, some more
- 2 teaspoons baking powder
- 8 ounces Oaxaca cheese
- 4 ounces Swiss cheese
- 4 large organic eggs
- 20 grams of heavy cream

Directions

1.Mix all the listed ingredients in a mixing bowl.

2.And knead it well.

3.Now line a parchment paper inside the Bundt pan.

4.Put the bowl mixture to pan

5.Place it in a cooking chamber at 400 degrees F for about 10 minutes in the air fryer.

6.Once done, remove it from the Instant Omni plus air fryer toaster oven and cool for 15 minutes before serving.

Nutrition Facts
Servings: 3
Amount per serving
Calories 658
% Daily Value*
Total Fat 35.6g 46%
Saturated Fat 21g 105%
Cholesterol 332mg 111%
Sodium 656mg 29%
Total Carbohydrate 47.3g 17%
Dietary Fiber 0.5g 2%
Total Sugars 1g
Protein 37.4g
Vitamin D 43mcg 217%
Calcium 1016mg 78%
Iron 2mg 10%
Potassium 460mg 10%

100

MARBLE CHEESECAKE

It is a very healthy recipe to enjoy.

Preparation Time: 25 Minutes

Cooking Time: 22minutes

Yield: 2 Servings

Ingredients

- 1 cup graham cracker crumbs
- 2 tablespoons softened butter
- 10 ounces Cream cheese softened
- 1/3 cup sugar
- 2 organic eggs
- 1 tablespoon flour
- 1 teaspoon vanilla extract
- 1/3 cup chocolate syrup

Directions

1.In a large bowl, mix the graham cracker and butter.

2.Press this mixture into a baking pan and refrigerate it for a few hours.

3.Meanwhile, combine the cream cheese and sugar.

4.Then add in the beaten egg.

5.Next, add the flour and vanilla.

6.Add the end add the chocolate syrup until combined.

7.Take out the pan from the refrigerator.

8.Pour this filling into the pan as a topping.

9.Bake it for 22 minutes at 320 degrees in an Instant Omni plus air fryer toaster oven.

10. Cool on a rack for 30 minutes, before serving.

11. Enjoy.

Nutrition Facts

Servings: 2

Amount per serving

Calories 858

% Daily Value*

Total Fat 27g 35%

Saturated Fat 6.3g 32%

Cholesterol 175mg 58%

Sodium 1389mg 60%

Total Carbohydrate 118.6g 43%

Dietary Fiber 6g 21%

Total Sugars 70.4g

Protein 38.1g

Vitamin D 15mcg 77%

Calcium 294mg 23%

Iron 7mg 40%

Potassium 617mg 13%

101

EGGLESS CAKE

It is a perfect sweet treat for all vegans out there.

Preparation Time: 15 Minutes

Cooking Time: 12 Minutes

Yields: 4 Servings

Ingredients

- 1/4 cup all-purpose flour
- 4 tablespoons sugar
- 2 tablespoons cocoa powder
- 1/8 teaspoon baking soda
- 3 teaspoon milk
- 2 tablespoons olive oil
- 2 tablespoons warm water
- 2 drops vanilla extract
- Pinch of salt
- 6 raw almonds

Directions

1. Take a bowl of medium size and add sugar, water, oil and milk.

2. Whisk them together to make a smooth better

3.Now put cocoa powder, salt, all-purpose flour, and baking soda to the batter and whisk again to make a smooth mixture.

4.Take (quiche pan) and transfer the batter. It must be a 4inch cake pan and should be buttered/ oiled.

5.Use chopped almonds as topping.

6.Put the baking skillet in the pre - heated Instant Omni plus air fryer toaster oven.

7.Allow air-frying for about 10 minutes at 330 degrees F.

8.Use a toothpick to make sure that the cake is entirely cooked.

9.Take out the pan and allow it to cool down.

10. Slice and enjoy after cooling.

Nutrition Facts

Servings: 4

Amount per serving

Calories 152

% Daily Value*

Total Fat 8.4g 11%

Saturated Fat 1.3g 7%

Cholesterol 0mg 0%

Sodium 80mg 3%

Total Carbohydrate 20g 7%

Dietary Fiber 1.2g 4%

Total Sugars 12.3g

Protein 1.8g

Vitamin D 0mcg 0%

Calcium 14mg 1%

Iron 1mg 5%

Potassium 92mg 2%

102

AIR FRYER BANANA BREAD

If you are banana bread lover then this recipe serves you well.

Preparation Time: 20 Minutes

Cooking Time: 30 Minutes

Yields: 4 Servings

Ingredients

- Cooking spray, for greasing
- 3/4 cup all-purpose flour
- 2 teaspoon ground cinnamon
- 1 teaspoon kosher salt
- 1/2 teaspoon baking soda
- 3 bananas, mashed
- 3 large eggs, beaten
- 1/4 cup white sugar
- 1/3 cup whole milk
- 3 tablespoons vegetable oil
- 1/3 teaspoon vanilla extract
- 3 tablespoons walnuts, chopped

Directions

1.Preheat the air fryer to 310 degrees F.

2.Coat a 6-inch circular cake pan with a cooking spray at the sides and bottom.

3.Whisk flour, salt, cinnamon, and baking soda in a bowl.

4.Take a separate bowl and mix vanilla extract, oil, milk, sugar, eggs, and bananas in it.

5.Mix this banana mixture into flour batter just until mixture is combined well; pour this batter into an already greased cake pan.

6.Dust walnuts over the top of batter.

7.Position cake pan in the chamber of Instant Omni plus air fryer toaster ovenand cook for about 30 minutes, until a toothpick comes out clean when placed in the center.

8.Move the bread to a wire rack for 15 minutes in pan to cool.

9.Take the bread off the plate and serve.

Nutrition Facts

Servings: 4

Amount per serving

Calories 408

% Daily Value*

Total Fat 18.7g 24%

Saturated Fat 3.9g 20%

Cholesterol 142mg 47%

Sodium 802mg 35%

Total Carbohydrate 53.4g 19%

Dietary Fiber 3.9g 14%

Total Sugars 24.9g

Protein 10.2g

Vitamin D 21mcg 106%

Calcium 66mg 5%

Iron 2mg 13%

Potassium 457mg 10%

103

AIR FRYER BANANA BREAD

It is a perfect bread recipe to enjoy.

Preparation Time: 25 Minutes

Cooking Time: 40 Minutes

Yields: 4 Servings

Ingredients

- 2 cups purpose flour
- Salt, pinch
- 1 teaspoon baking soda
- 2 ripe bananas
- 3 teaspoons granulated sugar
- 2 teaspoons vegetable oil
- 1 cup sour cream
- 2 pure vanilla extract
- 2 eggs
- 1 cup chopped walnuts

Directions

1.Take a bowl of large size; whisk the salt, flour, and baking soda together.

2.Take a medium size bowl and mash bananas in it until it turn very smooth. Use potato masher or fork to mash bananas.

3.Whisk in egg, vanilla, sour cream, oil, and sugar. Make sure that all items are perfectly smooth.

4.Mix this batter in dry ingredients and just combined with it. Do not do over-mixing.

5.Softly blend in walnuts if wanted.

6.Pour the mixture to a cake pan and put this pan inside of the basket in the Instant Omni plus air fryer toaster oven.

7.Bake this batter for 33 -37 minutes at 310 degrees F, or until the toothpick comes out clean.

8.Leave to cool down on a wire rack in the baking pan for about 20 minutes prior to removal.

Nutrition Facts

Servings: 4

Amount per serving

Calories 659

% Daily Value*

Total Fat 35.8g 46%

Saturated Fat 9.9g 49%

Cholesterol 107mg 36%

Sodium 417mg 18%

Total Carbohydrate 69.9g 25%

Dietary Fiber 5.4g 19%

Total Sugars 11g

Protein 19.2g

Vitamin D 8mcg 39%

Calcium 110mg 8%

Iron 4mg 25%

Potassium 554mg 12%

104

AIR FRYER PUMPKIN SPICE CUPCAKE

These are tender and crispy pumpkin spice muffins that are prepared in couple of minutes.

Preparation Time: 15 Minutes

Cooking Time: 12 Minutes

Yields: 2 Servings

Ingredients

- 1-1/2 Cup flour
- 1 tablespoon baking powder
- 1/2 Cup sugar
- 1 teaspoon vanilla extract
- 1 tablespoon pumpkin spice
- 1/3 Cup pumpkin puree
- 2 Eggs
- 1/2 Cup milk
- 3 tablespoons olive oil

Directions

1. In a muffin tray, put the muffin liners and set aside.

2. Combine sugar, baking powder and flour in a bowl.

3. Mix oil, milk, vanilla extract, egg, pumpkin puree, and pumpkin spice in another dish.

4.Blend in wet ingredients gradually with dry ingredients.

5.Whip until all is well blended and no bumps are left.

6.Share the mixture between the muffin liners and put them in the air fryer bowl.

7.Adjust the temperature to 360 degrees and air fry for 10-12 minutes, inside Instant Omni plus air fryer toaster oven.

8.Then serve.

Nutrition Facts

Servings: 2

Amount per serving

Calories 725

% Daily Value*

Total Fat 27.7g 36%

Saturated Fat 5.5g 27%

Cholesterol 169mg 56%

Sodium 102mg 4%

Total Carbohydrate 110.1g 40%

Dietary Fiber 3.5g 12%

Total Sugars 55.1g

Protein 14.6g

Vitamin D 16mcg 79%

Calcium 460mg 35%

Iron 5mg 30%

Potassium 1024mg 22%

105

AIR FRYER FRENCH BREAD PIZZA

It is a perfect pizza recipe that is scrumptious treat for dinner time, and it's prepared with easy.

Preparation Time: 15 Minutes

Cooking Time: 7 Minutes

Yields: 5 Servings

Ingredients

- 1 loaf French bread
- 1/2 jar pizza sauce, of choice
- 1/2 cup pepperonis, quartered
- 1/2 cup mozzarella cheese, less or more depending on preference
- 1 clove garlic, minced
- 1/4 cup butter
- Few leaves of basil, optional

Directions

1.Melt the 1/4-cup butter in a small pot.

2.Mix the butter with clove and garlic.

3.Cut the French bread loaf lengthwise and then cut in half. You will get four bread parts.

4.Brush the butter melted butter mixture onto the French bread.

5.Adjust the air fryer to 400 ° for 7 minutes.

6.Place the French sliced bread on the plates, and add when the Instant Omni plus air fryer toaster oven show add.

7.Cool for 4 minutes

8.Then serve.

Nutrition Facts

Servings: 6

Amount per serving

Calories 785

% Daily Value*

Total Fat 32.6g 42%

Saturated Fat 13.1g 66%

Cholesterol 73mg 24%

Sodium 1957mg 85%

Total Carbohydrate 91.4g 33%

Dietary Fiber 3.9g 14%

Total Sugars 4.3g

Protein 31g

Vitamin D 10mcg 49%

Calcium 102mg 8%

Iron 7mg 37%

Potassium 349mg 7%

106

PEPPERONI PIZZA BAKE

The pizza that is bake to its perfection, using Omni air fryer.

Preparation Time: 10 Minutes

Cooking Time: 15 Minutes

Yields: 2 Servings

Ingredients

- 1 package refrigerated biscuits
- 6 ounces pizza sauce
- 4 cups shredded mozzarella cheese
- 2 package pepperoni, slices

Directions

1.Oil sprays the non-stick pan in an air fryer.

2.Slice each dough of biscuit into eight parts.

3.Mix mozzarella cheese (1 cup) and pizza sauce together in a small dish.

4.Mix your dough of biscuit into the batter, and coat well.

5.When the dough is covered with the cheese/sauce, put it in the prepared pan.

6.Complete it all with the biscuit dough.

7.Use pepperoni pieces over the top.

8.Dust one cup of cheese over the pepperoni.

9.Put them in the Instant Omni plus air fryer toaster oven.

10. Adjust the temperature for 15 minutes, at 275 degrees F.

11. Check to ensure all of the dough is baked after the 15 minutes, if not allow to cook for additional 3 minutes.

12. Top up, serve and enjoy.

Nutrition Facts

Servings: 2

Amount per serving

Calories 607

% Daily Value*

Total Fat 36.9g 47%

Saturated Fat 14.9g 74%

Cholesterol 88mg 29%

Sodium 2185mg 95%

Total Carbohydrate 35.2g 13%

Dietary Fiber 2.2g 8%

Total Sugars 6.3g

Protein 33.2g

Vitamin D 5mcg 25%

Calcium 88mg 7%

Iron 4mg 21%

Potassium 231mg 5%

107

FROZEN PIZZA ROLLS

These are equally loved by kids and adults.

Preparation Time: 10 Minutes

Cooking Time: 3Minutes

Yields: 2 Servings

Ingredients

- 1 bag frozen pizza rolls

Directions

1.Place pizza roll on a cooking chamber, and place dripping pan on lower chamber to collect dripping.

2.Cook it for about 7 minutes, at 180 ° C/ 380 ° F, inside Instant Omni plus air fryer toaster oven.

3.While Three minutes are remaining in cooking time, turn all rolls of pizza.

4.Dish out, and enjoy.

Nutrition Facts

Servings: 2

Amount per serving

Calories 289

% Daily Value*

Total Fat 14.2g 18%

Saturated Fat 3.8g 19%
Cholesterol 23mg 8%
Sodium 651mg 28%
Total Carbohydrate 29.7g 11%
Dietary Fiber 1.7g 6%
Total Sugars 0g
Protein 10.8g
Vitamin D 0mcg 0%
Calcium 77mg 6%
Iron 0mg 0%
Potassium 0mg 0%

108

AIR FRYER GARLIC BREAD PIZZA TOAST

It is a perfect alternative to restaurant style pizza.

Preparation Time: 10 Minutes

Cooking Time: 5-6 Minutes

Yields: 5 Servings

Ingredients

- 10 slices of garlic bread, texas toast
- 1 jar of pizza sauce
- 14 ounces mozzarella cheese (shredded works great too)
- Few leaves basil

Directions

1.Put the drip pan in the cooking chamber's bottom. Tap AIRFRY with the display panel, then change the temperature to 380 degrees F, adjust the time to 6 minutes, and then tap START.

2.Add four pieces of texas toast on tray and put it on the bottom shelf when the screen suggests "Add Food" Then shut the door.

3.Allow cooking for about 2 minutes, so that the bottom will crisp up.

4.Open the door and flip toasts. Then shut the door.

5.Let it crisp for Two minutes.

6.Open the Instant Omni plus air fryer toaster oven door and scoop around two tablespoons of pizza sauce over the top of the toast

7.Put two slices of fresh mozzarella slices over the toast top.

8.Try to fit one or two leaves of basil between slices of cheese

9.Cook for 2 minutes and serve

Nutrition Facts

Servings: 5

Amount per serving

Calories 674

% Daily Value*

Total Fat 46.2g 59%

Saturated Fat 14.4g 72%

Cholesterol 42mg 14%

Sodium 1340mg 58%

Total Carbohydrate 37.6g 14%

Dietary Fiber 2.4g 9%

Total Sugars 2.8g

Protein 28.8g

Vitamin D 0mcg 0%

Calcium 64mg 5%

Iron 0mg 2%

Potassium 0mg 0%

109

CRISPY AIR FRYER EGGPLANT PARMESAN

It is a very yummy treat to enjoy.

Preparation Time: 16 Minutes

Cooking Time: 10 Minutes

Yields: 2 Servings

Ingredients

- 2 large eggplants
- 1 cup bread crumbs
- 5 tablespoons parmesan cheese
- Salt to taste
- 2 teaspoons Italian seasoning mix
- 5 tablespoons wheat flour
- 2 eggs, whisked
- 2 teaspoon water
- Olive oil spray
- 1 cup marinara sauce
- 1/2 cup grated mozzarella cheese
- Basil leaves, to garnish

Directions

1.Cut the eggplant into 1/2 inches slices approximately.

2.Sprinkle some salt from both slice's sides and stand for at least 10-15 minutes.

3.In the meantime, mix flour and water with egg to make the batter in a small dish.

4.Mix some salt, blend of Italian seasoning, parmesan cheese, and breadcrumbs in a medium shallow plate. Combine all ingredients carefully.

5.Now add the batter to every slice of an eggplant. Roll the battered slices to breadcrumb blend; be coated uniformly on all ends.

6.Put breaded slices of eggplant on a dry, clean flat plate and sprinkle oil on them.

7.The Instant Omni plus air fryer toaster oven is preheated to 360 degrees F.

8.Then place slices of eggplant on the tray, put in air fryer and bake for around 8 minutes.

9.Top these air fried slices with around one tablespoon of marinara sauce and spread the fresh mozzarella cheese lightly over them.

10. Cook the eggplant for the next 1-2 min just until the cheese has melted.

11. Serve warm.

Nutrition Facts

Servings: 2

Amount per serving

Calories 604

% Daily Value*

Total Fat 13.9g 18%

Saturated Fat 4.2g 21%

Cholesterol 172mg 57%

Sodium 1132mg 49%

Total Carbohydrate 98.6g 36%

Dietary Fiber 22.4g 80%

Total Sugars 28.5g

Protein 24.6g

Vitamin D 15mcg 77%
Calcium 230mg 18%
Iron 6mg 35%
Potassium 1630mg 35%

FRENCH BREAD

It is an easy bread recipe to enjoy with Omni air fryer toaster oven.

Preparation Time: 10 Minutes

Cooking Time: 6 Minutes

Yields: 3 Servings

Ingredients

- 1 can refrigerate French loaf dough
- 3 tablespoons butter, melted
- 3 tablespoons Bagel Seasoning

Directions

1. Start by removing dough from the bowl, and put it on a chopping board. Split the dough in two halves, I made two loaves, because of the size the used air fryer; I would use only 1/2 of the dough.

2. Put the loaf of bread, seams side down in the basket of the air fryer or onto the baking tray.

3. Heat up some butter, and then spread to the loaf using a pastry brush.

4. Spray all seasoning over the top of the untoasted crust.

5. Place your bread in the basket of Instant Omni plus air fryer

toaster oven, at 320 degrees F for six minutes. Whenever the time is up, confirm if it is done.

6.Tray, serves, and enjoy!

Nutrition Facts

Servings: 2

Amount per serving

Calories 227

% Daily Value*

Total Fat 18.2g 23%

Saturated Fat 11.2g 56%

Cholesterol 46mg 15%

Sodium 302mg 13%

Total Carbohydrate 14.3g 5%

Dietary Fiber 0.5g 2%

Total Sugars 1.2g

Protein 2.6g

Vitamin D 12mcg 60%

Calcium 5mg 0%

Iron 1mg 5%

Potassium 5mg 0%

CONCLUSION

Making easy, versatile, and delicious air fryer recipes are no longer a problem. This comprehensive guide provides you with all the information necessary to use Instant Omni plus air fryer toaster oven as a beginner. The recipes are presented in categories and snippets of nutritional information.

As a beginner, you will get all the necessary information to use the Instant Omni plus air fryer toaster oven to prepare the meals.

We hope you like our efforts.